Best Wine Buys

IN THE

High Street 1995

————

J U D Y R I D G W A Y

foulsham
LONDON • NEW YORK • TORONTO • SYDNEY

foulsham

The Publishing House, Cippenham, Berks., SL1 5AP

ISBN 0-572-02035-X

Printed in Great Britain by Cox & Wyman Ltd, Reading

Contents

Preamble

The range of wines on offer in the high street has never been greater, and despite the recession we are all buying more wine than ever before. One of the reasons for this is the increasing number of drinkable wines on sale which manage to creep under the all-important £3.00 barrier (apparently we are not prepared to pay very much more than this for our everyday wine).

This low level of pricing is achieved mainly on red wines from the Vin de Pays regions of France, and from non-classic areas of Spain, Italy and Bulgaria. The wines are light but mostly have good, fruity flavours. Good white wine is more difficult to find at this price and you will probably have to pay between £3.00 and £3.50 for something with any character.

One of the reasons for the upsurge in the quality of wines at the cheaper end of the market is the influence of a new wave of young (mainly New World) wine-makers who are rushing from one wine-making area to another offering advice and technical know-how. These so-called 'flying wine-makers' are also leading the way in Eastern Europe where Hungary in particular is producing excellent wines at reasonable prices. The problem is that no one really knows how producers in Eastern Europe are managing to keep their finances on the go and there could be some casualties, so enjoy these wines while you can.

The flying wine-makers are undoubtedly making a real difference to the high street wine market, but there are those who complain that they are perpetuating our love affair with Chardonnay and Cabernet Sauvignon grapes at the expense of indigenous grapes which could, if given the same treatment, produce really interesting wines in their own right.

To some extent the choice is up to us. If we continue to ignore wines made from lesser known grape varieties in favour of the ever-popular top two, that is eventually all we will get.

Chardonnay is currently the magic word on a white wine label, but line up five or six Chardonnay wines and you will have a range of different flavours. Chardonnay from the Italian Trentino does not taste the same as Chardonnay from Hungary, Vin de Pays d'Oc or Chile - to name but a few. Some are good some are not, but they all command a premium over other (and to my mind equally interesting) grape varieties.

For me the range of choice is part of the many attractions of good wine, but it can be a little daunting. Most supermarkets now stock literally hundreds and hundreds of wines from all over the world. Where do you start?

This is, of course, the question I hope to address for you in this book. I spend many hours each year tasting wine and can now claim to have tasted virtually all the wines listed here. I have included all styles of wine so that there should be something to suit everyones's taste. Those which I think are particularly good value in their style and price range or which I particularly like are marked with an asterisk.

Changes in the price is a problem area for a book like this and so I have set out the prices in price bands £2.00-2.50, £2.50-3.00, and so on. These were as accurate as they could be at the time of going to press.

Vintages can be another problem area for a book like this, but because most of the wines in the book should be drunk fairly young I have decided not to bother with them. This also means that the book is not out of date once the supplies from one year run out and another vintage is substituted in the shops.

Quite often the same producers achieve consistently high scores in my tasting notes. This is because a good producer will make as good a wine as is possible in the bad years and superlatively good wines in the good years. (It is worth trying to remember the names of the producers of those wines which you really like).

Most supermarkets now have helpful shelf notes which tell you a little more about the wines on offer and some also highlight wines which have been mentioned by leading wine-writers. You will also see references to various medals and certificates of excellence. These can be quite helpful, provided that you understand the basis on which they are awarded.

First, producers, importers or retailers usually have to pay to enter their wines for consideration by the panel of judges. Some can afford to put in a large numbers, others cannot. The judging is usually done by a panel of five or six or more people (all wine specialists of various kinds) who may or may not be particular experts in the style of wine being judged. The result is judgement by committee and the awards often a compromise.

Remember that at the end of the day it is what you like that counts, so don't be afraid to trust your own judgement. Be adventurous, try different wines and have fun making up your own mind about what you want to drink.

First steps towards a choice

The price, the occasion and the taste are the three criteria used most when choosing and buying wine. These decisions are usually made in the shop. Okay, you may sometimes decide in advance that you just have to have a bottle of Chablis or claret but more often than not my shopping list simply specifies 'wine', without any mention of appellation, style or area.

Perhaps the most important criterion today is the price tag. The vast majority of wines that are sold in the high street still fall into the £2.50-3.50 range and supermarket managers tell me that sales fall off dramatically after the £4.00 mark. Indeed in these years of recession customers generally have been buying wine priced under £3.00 a bottle. Price is important, but, if you possibly can pay more, you can benefit much more than proportionally by moving up the price ladder (see page 13 to see why).

The next criterion is the food and the occasion. The question is not which Rousillon or Chianti shall I have, but which wine shall I buy to serve at that Sunday barbecue or to drink on an evening at home? I believe that this is so important that I have included a special section on matching food and wine (see pages 23–29).

The third, and possibly equally important, criterion is what will it taste like? Some shops do help here by using the Wine Promotion Board's taste guides. These are a combination of symbols and numbers (white wine) or letters (red wine) which give you some indication of the sweetness levels in white wine and the body of red wine.

You will probably have an idea of what some wines taste like simply from having tried them before. You may also know a little about what a particular grape variety might taste like or what style to expect from a particular wine-growing region or a fortified wine such as sherry or port. You may even have read the chapters at the end of this book on how wine is made and where it comes from. But at the end of the day you will still be dependent upon the labelling.

Understanding descriptions

In some shops there are no shelf descriptions and the only information is on the label. This rarely spells out the character of the wine in so many words. You can see the colour, but will it make light and easy drinking - the sort of thing that you are looking for for a party? Or, will it be the kind of full-bodied and warming wine you need to offset your special spiced pork casserole?

The clues are on the label, so look at it carefully before buying. All labels will tell you which country the wine comes from and may tell you which region within that country. Thus, if you have drunk an Italian Valpolicella with your lasagne or a Listel Gris de Gris with your Salade Niçoise and found that the combinations worked, you should easily find them again.

For countries which have an appellation or classification system, the label will tell you whether the contents of the bottle are of the basic easy-drinking, party wine variety or are 'fine' wines from prestigious regions or estates. The price will also probably tell you this too!

Other useful information can come from the stated alcohol levels. Light wines like those from Germany, come in at the 8-9.5 per cent alcohol by volume level, whereas some of the red wines of Italy reach 13.5-14 per cent levels. Obviously the latter will need a fair amount of food to offset the alcohol alone.

An indication of quality may also be given in the small print at the base of the label. It will tell you here if the wine is an EU blend, if it is bottled hundreds of kilometres away from the region in which it was produced, or if it was bottled at the estate where it was made (see page 155).

Some wines are labelled by their grape variety (those from Alsace, California, Australia and Chile, for example) and this can be useful in giving an indication, at least, of the kind of flavours to expect.

Once you have tasted a Sauvignon Blanc from Touraine and one from California, or perhaps Australia, you will have a better idea of what to expect from bottles labelled Sauvignon Blanc in the future.

Labels also carry a certain amount of 'hype'. Growers are fond of words like 'reserve', 'special' and 'cuvée'. Sometimes they mean something, sometimes they don't! For more information on this and on labels generally, consult the sections on the various wine-producing countries at the back of this book.

If you are not familiar with the different styles of the various wine-producing countries and the effect that different methods of production and ageing can have on the wine, look to see if there is a back label on the bottle.

These potentially helpful notes first appeared on wines from California and Australia. Some of them do need a degree in wine-making to decipher them, but the better ones tell you about the grape varieties used and the resultant style of the wine and how tannic, acid or oaky it is. They often include helpful serving suggestions as well.

Most of the supermarkets have cleverly taken up the idea for their own-label wines and they produce back labels which are both informative and easy to understand.

Wine language

Some supermarkets and off-licence chains are making great efforts to increase the flow of information on wine. There are short descriptions on the shelves above or below the wine racks and they have produced wine lists and booklets describing the wines. Which brings us to the subject of 'winespeak'.

There are three approaches to the language used to describe wine. First of all there is the fairly straightforward approach which attempts to give a general description of what's in the bottle.

Words such as full, fruity, rich, young, strong and flowery are but a few. Some also try to give a short comparative description of the flavours, such as blackcurrant, gooseberries, bramble jam and minty.

Of course, the wine doesn't actually taste exactly like the description, but is reminiscent of it ... though now I come to think of it some Aussie Cabernets do taste exactly like fresh blackcurrants!

Provided these descriptions do not go too far, they can be very helpful and they are the standard language of the supermarket shelves. (See pages 9–10 for a list of some of the most commonly used phrases.)

Once the language starts to go beyond these frontiers, we

are definitely in the land of winespeak. There is an on-going controversy among avid readers of the specialist wine magazines. On the one hand there are those who enjoy the flights of fancy of some writers and revel in phrases such as 'sweaty saddles', 'cat's pee', 'new mown hay' and 'autumn leaf mould'.

Those in the opposing camp are the third group who say that all these descriptions are, at best, pure flights of fancy and, at worst, sheer pretension. They prefer to enjoy the merits of their wine in silence!

As a wine writer, I have mixed feelings. If I am enthusiastic about a wine I want to convey my pleasure in its taste to other people and some sort of description seems to be the only way. But will my listeners or readers find the same flavour comparisons that I do? Perhaps the really flowery descriptions are best kept as an *aide-mémoire* for our own taste memories.

A guide to the meaning of common descriptions

Acidity: This gives zest and freshness to a wine and helps to balance sweeter wines which would just be cloying without it. It sometimes tastes rather like raw cooking apples, at others more like lemon or grapefruit juice. Too much acidity is unpleasant.

Baked: A 'hot' rather jammy or earthy smell or taste produced when the grapes have been grown in excessive sunshine with low rainfall.

Balance: This is the very important ratio between all the different characteristics of the wine, such as fruit, acidity, tannin and alcohol. These should all harmonise to give a rounded effect.

Body: This refers to the feel of the wine in the mouth due both to the fullness of flavour and the level of alcohol. It may be described as light or full.

Character: This indicates that the wine has a distinctive style to it.

Closed: This is a wine which does not smell or taste as much as you would expect. It may not be mature enough.

Complex: A wine with many facets.

Crisp: Often a euphemism for very acidic.

Elegant: A stylish and refined quality; the opposite of opulent.

Flowery: This usually means the wine has a fragrant, perfumed and flower-like aroma and flavour.

Fresh: This is a wine which retains its youthful acidity.

Fruity: This overworked word refers to the prominent flavour of the grapes, but it does not necessarily mean grapey as in the flavour of fresh table grapes.

Honeyed: This is a characteristic of some white wines and is often intensified with age.

Oaky: This is a flavour imparted to the wine from ageing in oak barrels. It has a distinctive vanilla-like smell.

Pétillant: This is a very slight degree of natural sparkle. It shows as tiny bubbles on the side of the glass and a faint prickle on the tongue.

Soft: This usually means that the acidity levels of the wine are quite low.

Tannin: This gives a furry, rather harsh impression on the gums and teeth. Some tannin can be very pleasant, too much is not. A tannic wine may soften with age.

And finally a couple of words which you are unlikely to find on a wine list, but which may be useful to know:

Corked: This does not mean that there are bits of crumbled cork in the wine, but refers to wine which has a very distinctive smell and taste of mould or decaying wood. It is caused by a fungal infection of the cork.

Oxidised or maderised: These terms refer to wine which has been spoilt by exposure to air. The latter term is used more often in connection with white wine. The wine has a characteristic slightly sherry-like taste and a darker than usual colour.

Dry or sweet?

These are two words which do mean something (though not always the same thing) to everyone. The level of sweetness is one of the most important flavour characteristics of a wine.

You probably have a very definite idea of how dry or how sweet you like your wine to be. You may also know that Muscadet and Chablis are pretty dry and that Liebfraumilch and Lambrusco are on the sweeter side. But do you know exactly where Vinho Verde, Soave, Australian Rhine Riesling or Anjou Rosé come on the sweetness/dryness scale?

To save you having to remember exactly where each wine comes in relation to another, the Wine Development Board has drawn up a guide to the sweetness of white wines. It is based on a simple nine-point scale with 1 as very dry and 9 as very sweet (see page 37).

Many supermarkets and off-licence chains put the symbols and numbers on their shelves. Use them to find your way round areas which are new to you or in experimenting with different wines. Don't just stick at the same sweetness level, try wines from some of the other levels as well. This advice refers as much to those who usually buy at number 1 on the scale, as to those who buy at number 4 or 5. Most of us are too blinkered in our choice of wine.

There seems to be a view that dry white wine is the most sophisticated and the best choice. People who like sweeter wines are made to feel that they should apologise for their tastes. This is quite wrong.

It is just not true that dry is best. It depends on the individual wine concerned. Some dry white wines are astringent and unpleasant and if you strike one of these in your first foray into drier wines, it will not be surprising if you are put off. Conversely there are some sweet wines which do not have enough acidity to offset the sugar and these can be quite cloying and unpleasant.

However, there are first-class wines at all levels of the scale and the dry wine snob is losing out on a fair amount of enjoyment. So, keep an open mind and drink around!

Vintages

How important are vintages? Not very important at the table wine level (they don't usually carry a date anyway). These wines will often be blends designed to eradicate the vagaries of the weather in particular areas. Some of them are branded wines and the wine-makers here too are looking for consistency of flavour and achieve it by blending.

Even at the Vin de Pays level the vintage is not all that important. All these wines are made to be drunk young and though you may detect a slight difference from year to year, no-one is planning to keep them.

At the Appellation Contrôlé level the vintage must be stated on the bottle. For us high street wine-buyers this can be useful, but not critical. If you read that the Loire wines have done badly one year, you may switch to Pinot Grigio or La Mancha for a while.

On the other hand a series of good vintages in Bordeaux, for example, will mean that quality wine will be available even at the lowest levels. It may also be worth buying in a stock of a good vintage to keep for a year or two. Wines which are worth keeping include reds from Burgundy, Bordeaux, the Loire and the Rhône as well as red wines from Tuscany (Chianti) and Piedmonte (Barolo). Some New World wines will also improve with a year or two in bottle.

It is really only if you are thinking of buying some older vintages (very expensive even if you can find them), or planning to buy wine '*en primeur*' (before it has been bottled) and keep it for a few years that vintages become really important.

Fine red wines and a few white wines, such as white Burgundy (Meursault and Montrachet and even Chablis), Sauternes and German Rieslings at the Auslese level need longer ageing and if you are going to invest in them, it makes sense to start with the best years.

Vintages are often more important in Europe than they are in Australia or California, for there is much greater variation in the weather conditions there.

The problem now arises of deciding which is a good vintage. Reports pour out of the various wine-growing regions during the year, culminating in a positive deluge at and after the harvest. The problem is that according to these no region has a *very* bad time and every nearby grower has had a much worse time than the one producing the report.

Independent reports from journalists and the like are not all the much better, though a year hailed as 'the vintage of the century' (a common occurrence these days) will probably end up being quite good. The point which is often forgotten is that the wine goes on developing and maturing until it is drunk and some years which have been written off by the pundits produce very pleasant wines eight or ten years later.

The other problem is that vintage assessments are far too general. They can only give a broad indication of the *average* level of quality. Individual wines may be much better or much worse and you really need to know your grower for detailed assessment.

Assessing prices

This book is concerned with wines priced under £5.00 (except for sparkling wines and special occasion wines). These are the wines which most people buy and, despite rising prices, there are still very many good wines in this category.

Expensive wine is usually good wine, but it is not necessarily the best wine. Much of it has a snob value or has become a fashion fad - like some of the Italian 'designer' Vino da Tavola wines.

Costly wines are fine to buy if you want to splash out for some reason, perhaps to impress a potential customer or even the boss. Or you may want to enjoy the opulent feeling of drinking something which is normally reserved for the very rich.

Celebrations, anniversaries and Christmas also merit a bit of extra expenditure and a good bottle of Champagne is very often the answer. For the rest of the time a cheaper wine will do very nicely, but how cheap? There are still a few wines in the £2.00-2.50 price range and rather more in the £2.50-3.00 range, but by and large it is really very difficult to find very many interesting wines under £3.00. Below this price the wines are usually fairly well made, but they are boring. This is particularly true of white wines.

At prices under £3.00 very, very little of the money is going to the grower or wine-producer. Most of it goes to the taxman and the middleman. So, the amount spent on the raw material (the wine) is minimal. A relatively small increase in price (50p or so) more than doubles the money going to the producer and there is a big leap in the quality of the wine you get.

Buying wine solely on price is a big mistake. If you possibly can pay 50p or even £1.00 more and you will experience the difference in the smell and taste of the wine.

Looking for bargains on the other hand obviously makes sense and there are bargains to be had. First of all there are 'loss leaders', otherwise known as monthly special offers. These are wines which have been reduced in price to tempt you into the shop in the hope that you will continue to buy there and maybe even buy some of the wines not on special offer. It's just the same as the cut-price canned beans in the supermarket. Because of slackening sales during the recession these monthly offers seem to be on the increase and they are well worth buying.

'Bin ends', or wines which have almost run out, are sold off cheap for a quick sale to make room for a new line. These may sometimes be wines which have not been as popular as expected and the shop wants to get shot of them. No problem for you if you happen to like them. On the other hand they may be wines which are beginning to reach their 'drink by date'!

Other wines are bought in quantity for the merchant to make his profit on high volume sales, and there are many more reasons for bargain offers.

These bargain offers are usually real bargains. Really bad wine is seldom put on offer. Some wines may be a little tired so check the vintages but there is too much risk to reputation and subsequent business in selling rubbish. So keep your eyes open and grab a bargain bottle when you see it. Try it quickly to see if you like it and rush back to buy more before everyone has discovered how good it is.

At certain times of the year, such as Christmas or the summer season, wines are reduced in price to catch extra trade. This is also the time to buy in more than you usually buy. If you are not sure where or how to store bottles at home, turn to pages 138–9.

Organic wine

The idea of a 'green' approach to the environment has taken a strong hold in the fields of packaging, domestic appliances and even food. But wine has largely escaped the trend. As yet the demand for ingredients or additive labelling is not very strong but there are demands for sulphur levels to be indicated. Given the EU food legislation it can only be a matter of time before such labelling in introduced.

In the meantime those who are interested in all things organic can now find wines which should come within their framework. The number of companies specialising in importing organic wines has risen to 12 or thereabouts and some of the supermarkets, strongly led by **Safeways** are also endeavouring to offer an organic choice on their wine shelves.

Indeed the subject of growing vines organically, without the use of chemical fertilisers and pesticides, is catching on with some growers, particularly in Germany, even more than it has with their consumers. France leads the field, closely followed by Germany and Italy. Spain and Portugal are just not interested. A few excellent organic wines are also coming in from New Zealand, Australia and California.

So what exactly is an organic wine? The easy answer is that if all chemicals have to be avoided it does not exist. Wine requires the use of sulphur to keep it in good condition and the few wines which are made without its use must be drunk within a few months of the harvest; by March or April the following year it is starting to tire and oxidise.

Until last year there were no generally agreed criteria for labelling organic wine but that has now changed with the introduction by the EU of Resolution 2092/91. This Resolution sets out rules governing the production of organically cultivated agricultural food stuffs and this, of course, includes wine.

Each country within the EU is required to set up a body to implement the regulations and to liaise with all those organisations which are concerned with things organic. In France there are 16 and in Germany almost as many. Here the regulating body is the United Kingdom Register of Organic Standards (UKROFS). Growers and producers have to register with a recognised organisation such as the Soil Association. Independent organic growers will be outlawed unless they sign up directly with the national implementation body itself.

The EU regulations are based largely on the experiences and existing practices of bodies like the Soil Association in the UK, Nature et Progres in France and Bioland in Germany. The standards should at long last be unified and have official sanction. We will know that what we are buying conforms to a set of rules backed up by an inspection system.

Each national body should accept those producers registered with their counterparts in other countries. This could cause some problems as there are organic associations whose standards have not been accepted outside their own countries. Another problem lies in the plethora of organic symbols. Each organic organisation has its own symbol and the national regulating bodies may also add their own. The answer would be a single European symbol but that is probably some way off. In the meantime we will have to continue to rely on our specialist importer to choose the best of the organic wines.

For the first time, the regulations also look at the processing of organic products. To use the term 'organic' on a processed product all additives or processes used in getting from raw ingredient to prepared product must feature on an approved list of substances and they must not make up more than 5 per cent of the total. So far wine is exempt from this part of the regulations. The submissions were so complicated that it will take some time for new organic wine laws to be formulated.

The regulations came into force in January 1993 but in practice only applies to wine produced and bottled after that date. The correct terminology on the label is 'wine made from organically grown grapes'. But it looks as if the term 'organic wine' will remain if it is explained somewhere on the label.

The line between organic and the best of the rest has been blurred to say the least and it will probably remain that way despite the regulations. There are plenty of ecologically sound vineyards, where artificial help is kept to a minimum and where the wines are naturally stable. On the other hand organic producers are still able to use sulphur. Nevertheless the levels are kept to a minimum and if you are asthmatic or known to be sensitive to sulphur it could be worth the extra cost of organic wine.

Yes, you will probably have to pay more for organic wines. The organic wine-maker has a hard task. He is attempting to make modern wines for modern tastes without the benefit of modern chemicals. This can be both labour intensive and extremely chancy.

So what do organic wines taste like? In my opinion they are as 'mixed a bag' as any group of wines. I have had some very poor organic wines and some very odd ones. Some have made me question my ideas of what a wine from a particular area should taste like. But I have also had some first-class organic wines which seemed to have extracted even more wonderful fruit flavours than are usually encountered in first-class wine.

Like all wine, it's a case of try it and see. A good opportunity to do just that is the Organic Wine Fair held at Ryton Gardens every July.

Here are some addresses and telephone numbers of wine merchants specialising in organic wines:

Haughton Fine Wines, Chorley, Nantwich, Cheshire CW5 8JR. Tel: 0270 74537.

HDRA, National Centre for Organic Gardening, Ryton-on-Dunsmore, Coventry CV8 3LG. Tel: 0203 303517.

The Organic Wine Company, PO Box 81, High Wycombe, Bucks HP13 5QN. Tel: 0494 446557.

Organics, 290a Fulham Palace Road, London SW6 6HP. Tel: 071 381 9924. (Italian wine specialist)

Real Foods Ltd, 37 Broughton Street, Edinburgh EH1 3JU. Tel: 031 557 1911.

Rodgers Fine Wines, 37 Ben Bank Road, Silkstone Common, Barnsley, South Yorks S75 4PE. Tel: 0226 790794. (German wine specialist)

Vinceremos Wines, 65 Raglan Road, Leeds, West Yorks LS2 9DZ. Tel: 0532 431691.

Vintage Roots, Sheeplands Farm, Wargrave Road, Wargrave, Berks RG10 8DT. Tel: 0734 401222.

Whitakers Wines, 8 Market Place, Buxton, Derbyshire SKl7 6EB. Tel: 0298 70241.

Some of the supermarkets and high street off-licence chains are also starting to offer organic wines. **Safeways** for example, has a range of ten wines. Some organic wines have been included in the listings on pages 36–130. See **Asda, Bottoms Up, House of Townend, Marks and Spencer, Morrisons, Oddbins, Safeways, Tesco** and **Waitrose**.

Branded wines

These are wines which are likely to taste the same from year to year. They are designed to do so. Having achieved this the wine-maker then proceeds to advertise the brand so that when we walk into a wine store, there will be at least one or two wines we know.

This is not necessarily to be condemned. Most of the branded wines are well made, even if they are sweeter than the connoisseur's choice and rather more expensive than similar wines which are not branded.

Everyone knows, I think, that Blue Nun is a blended Liebfraumilch and those who buy it know what to expect and will not be disappointed. It is a safe buy. Sichel, the makers of Blue Nun, have spent a lot of money ensuring that it will be so. The quality of the grapes used is very high and the quality control extremely sophisticated.

Piat d'Or and Mouton Cadet operate on the same principle. If you are in a crowded shops when the assistants have no time to help you or you are wading through a badly designed wine-list in a restaurant, the familiar name will come to your rescue.

However, you should be aware that you are paying for this peace of mind. Advertising and clever marketing costs money and that expense will certainly be passed on to you, the buyer. Nor should you believe all the ads tell you. Those for one of these well-known brands would have you believe that in France the wine is a French favourite. In fact I saw it in a Calais supermarket displayed under the sign 'Vins sans Frontiers' with a small collection of wines from outside France!

So, my advice is to buy a branded wine you know and like if you are in a hurry, but when you have a little time to spare to talk to the shop assistant or to browse along the labels and make the effort to try something else in the same price range. You will probably get a much more interesting wine.

Boxes, tins and cartons

Modern packaging methods are here to stay and they have their uses. Canned wine is handy when on a picnic or snacking away from home. The wine does not seem to suffer from contact with the tin's lining and the quality is acceptable. Rather more attractive are the small glass bottles holding 250 cl which are just beginning to appear in the supermarkets. **Safeway**, for example, have a selection.

Cartons are less popular then they used to be. They are difficult to open and to pour. You cannot re-close them if you don't drink up all the contents.

Wine boxes, on the other hand, are very useful for parties and for people who only want to drink a glass or two at a time, but like to have a supply on hand. (Though these people might be better off investing in one of the new bottle seals.)

The wine in wine boxes is variable. Some of it is pretty ordinary, some is average and some is quite good. If you encounter one of the better ones at a friend's party, jot down the name before you forget and buy it in for yourself in the future. A good example is **Tesco**'s Chardonnay Domaine des Fontaines which costs £9.79 for 2 litres.

It was often thought when wine boxes were first introduced that the wine was cheaper. In fact, a comparison with the same wine in the bottle often shows that you are paying the same, if not more, volume for volume, for the larger-sized carton.

And the wine does not keep for ever. Two to three weeks really is the maximum time you should keep the wine after the carton box has been opened. Take care when fiddling with the tap - this is where air can start to creep in.

The French option

The Customs and Excise Duty rules and regulations changed quite drastically in January 1993 and you can now bring home greatly increased amounts of beer, wine and spirits provided that it is bought duty-paid in an EU member country.

The Customs guidelines suggest that the limits are set at 90 litres of table wine and 20 litres of fortified or sparkling wine. But in fact there are no legal limits; the proviso is that the wine should be for your own personal use and not for re-sale. Quite large quantities of beer and spirits can be brought in at the same time. So if you are planning a celebration, an anniversary party or a wedding it will certainly pay you to take a trip to France.

The easiest way to take advantage of the change in the law is to take the car to France and to stock up in northern France. This worked very well for beer and spirits but last year it was not so good for wine. The range of choice and, even more importantly, the quality of wine in French supermarkets was and indeed still is not as good as that in the UK.

But as the rush to save the duty grew so wine merchants both here and in France realised that there was a killing to be made and the number of outlets selling wine within reasonable reach of Calais has more than doubled. Some of the original French outlets continue to offer the same kind limited choice and quality that they did before the bonanza, but others have started to increase their ranges.

In addition, UK based firms have opened up shops and wine warehouses of their own and these have a great advantage because you can try the wines at home before buying in quantity in France.

Outlets fall into four major categories:

FRENCH SUPERMARKETS

There are five big supermarkets in the Calais area: Mammouth, Continent, Intermarche, Hyper Cedico and P&G and four near to Boulogne: Auchan, Intermarche, Leclerc and PG. Most of these supermarkets display a vast array of bottles but the actual choice of wine is not as wide as it looks. Bordeaux dominates with wines ranging from Vin de Table wines at around £1.30 a bottle to fine estate wines costing as much as £40 or more. There tend to be fewer white wines than red.

Sadly the really cheap wines in most of these supermarkets are either very tough and tannic or downright nasty. One or two of them might just pass muster with food but there is no real value for money here. Nor do the fine wines offer any savings. They can often be bought cheaper and in better condition in wine merchants back home!

The problem is that French people often buy wines simply because they have the right name on the label. This means that French supermarkets can get away with selling some truly bad wines labelled as Chablis, St Emilion or Sauternes which would be turned down flat by customers in British supermarkets.

The wines at similar prices to those we normally buy in the UK are probably the best bet. Two to three pounds will buy you a reasonable Vin de Pays Muscadet or Alsace Riesling. At home these would be at least 50p to a £1.00 more. Champagne is often a good buy too. There are some wines from other areas such as the Rhône or Languedoc and the quality of these is much better than it was last year.

AT P&G (a supermarket patronised by the French locals) the range is wider than most with red wines from a number of non-classic areas plus a reasonable number of white wines. Overall the quality is much the same but the prices are slightly lower. **Tesco** has an interest in Hyper Cedico and the store now offers some own-label wines. Mammoth is very good for reasonable Grande Meergie Champagnes.

See pages 125–130 for best buys from the French supermarkets.

UK SUPERMARKET WINE SHOPS

Sainsbury's was the first UK supermarket wine department to open up in France. They have taken a good-sized unit at the entrance to the shopping mall of the Mammoth hypermarket on the Boulogne side of Calais. You can select from an extensive range of 250 wines from around the globe and there is a good chance that your favourite JS wine will be on sale. The savings come from the fact that you will not be paying UK duty on the wine as the prices reflect the lower French duty.

Tesco will soon be following suit with a unit in Cite Europe, the new shopping centre, which is being built at the Channel Tunnel Terminal. This opens in January 1995 and Tesco's range of wines is expected to include virtually all the wines which are on sale in the UK.

INDEPENDENT WINE SHOPS AND WINE WAREHOUSES

These are springing up like mushrooms all over northern France. They vary from very small basic outlets like Easenders in Calais to much more sophisticated shops such as Les Chais and The Grape Shop in Boulogne. The latter company offers its customers the facility of tasting and ordering wines in London to be picked up and paid for in France. In Calais, one of the best shops is Le Bar au Vin near to the Hotel Bellevue. This shop sells fine wines at fairly reasonable prices. Another good shop is InterCave. This is one of a chain of shops which are independently owned but supplied by a central buying operation. They must have the largest assortment of bag-in-box wines in all France. They have branches in Calais, St Malo and Cherbourg.

Warehouse operations include La Maison du Vin, set up near to the port in Cherbourg by the Dorset company of the same name, Les Caves de Roscoff near the Plymouth ferry terminal, The Wine and Beer Warehouse in Calais run by Marco's wines of London, Champagne Charlie's and B n B Cash and Carry and Grand Crus Magnums also in Calais.

The Wine Society also offers its customers the chance to order in the UK and collect from their French suppliers at Hesdin in northern France (about 72 kilometres drive from Calais).

BUYING WINE IN NORTHERN FRANCE

It is easy to carried away by the low prices in the shops and supermarkets in northern France. But the fact that a wine has a Bordeaux château name on the label does not mean that it is a good wine. Nor does the fact that you can now buy wines from outside France mean that you will necessarily be getting a bargain.

* Avoid the temptation to think that the larger the outlet the cheaper the wine will be. This is just not so. There are cheap wines everywhere - the problem is to discover which are the good ones.

* If you possibly can, try a bottle or two before you buy in quantity. There is nothing worse than buying a cheap wine and finding that you have three or four cases of something which gets more and more awful with every bottle you open.

* Do not buy the cheapest wine just because it is the cheapest. If you do not know the wine check the label to see if it has won any medals (Medaille) at local wine competitions.

* Make a list of the wines which you generally drink and make a note of the price you pay in the UK. It is quite easy to forget what you actually pay at home and this will help you to see if you really are getting a bargain.

BUYING WINE IN THE WINE-GROWING REGIONS

Of course the new custom regulations do not just apply to wines bought in Calais, they embrace the whole of France and every EU country. So if you are on holiday, the sun is shining and the food and wine are going down a treat you might well think that this is the time to take advantage of the new duty-paid allowances.

However, it is one thing to enjoy a young and slightly rough local wine in the euphoria of a summer holiday, but quite another to serve it to your friends on a chilly evening in late October. Somehow the wine just does not taste the same.

The answer is only to buy quality wine. This may seem expensive on the face of it but can be a lot cheaper than it would be in the UK. If you are not staying in a wine-growing area it can be difficult to find a specialist wine merchant - they are much fewer on the ground than here - but you may come across an

InterCave or a Nicholas wine shop. If you like the wine on the hotel list you could ask the manager to introduce you to his merchant.

In the wine-growing areas it is of course easy to find wine - many of the growers offer tastings and sell from their own premises. This is fine in a white wine area or in an area where the wine is designed to be drunk young. But in the classic fine wine areas you will be tasting wine which is not yet ready to drink and most of the wine, good or bad, will not taste very pleasant when it is young.

However, if you are keen to buy on holiday, do some homework first. Make a list of the growers or shippers in the area you are going to whose wines you have tasted and enjoyed; and stick to these.

Buying duty-free wine

Incidently, if you are travelling to and from the Continent you may bring in a duty-free allowance purchased at the airport or on the plane or boat. This is in addition to the allowances of duty-paid wine outlined above.

Passengers crossing to the Continent by ferry may buy their duty-free allowance on the outward journey plus an identical allowance on the return journey and bring both sets of purchases into the country together. The old rules allowed only one set of duty-free purchases to be brought in. The new rules apply to day trips as well as to longer stays, but you must get off the boat at Calais.

What wine with food?

Wine and food are natural partners. But should you be drinking particular wines with particular foods? The enthusiastic 'foodie' will probably say yes. But in most cases the wines you fancy will go with the foods you like.

It is true that some partnerships work better than others and in an ideal world the wine and food should so enhance each other that both are improved. But most of us do not have the time or the wine stocks to make the ideal match at every meal.

Instead, we have to consider whether the chilli con carne will swamp our best wine or the plate of salami and olives needs a wine with plenty of acidity.

In the days of elaborate four, five and six course dinners rules were developed about what wines went with which food. White wine came to partner the fish course and red wine went with the meat course.

Today, meals are simpler and most people are unlikely to serve more than one wine at a meal unless it is a very special occasion. So, the chosen wine has to cope with very much more than it would have done before.

And if there are rules, we know they are there to be broken. After all the French, Spanish and Italians all cook fish in red wine and serve sweet wine with rich pâtés and blue cheeses.

So, where do you start? There are so many wines from which to choose and so many different ways of serving a simple food that any kind of analysis looks fraught with difficulty.

Here are some questions to ask yourself to help sort things out to start with:

Is the dish plainly cooked?   If it is, it will probably show off your best wines very well. The food and wine will not be fighting for attention and the flavour of the wine will not be swamped.

Is the main ingredient of the dish itself a fairly fatty or oily one? Good acidity in the wine is the answer here. Italian wines are often thought to be very acidic, but they are specifically designed to partner the rich Italian cuisine.

Is the dish particularly strongly flavoured or spicy?   Here   you have a choice: one answer is to choose a full rich wine, hopefully with complementary flavours. The other is to retreat into a fresh, but simple, wine which will allow the food to shine.

Does the dish have sweet or fruit flavours of its own?   If it does, you should choose a slightly sweeter wine. Completely dry wines can taste very astringent when there is sugar present in the meal. Sometimes you are able to match the fruity flavours in the wine with those of the dish.

Does the dish have a well-flavoured sauce?   Wines with a lower level of tannin, such as Burgundy, tend to go better with sauces than the tannic wines of Bordeaux, Piedmonte or Tuscany.

What are the component flavours of the dish?   Here you can try and match the flavours with those you find in different wines.

It is possible to go on analysing combinations to the nth degree and still end up arguing whether a German Riesling Spätlese from the Rheingau partnered your smoked salmon roulade with smoked trout mousse better than an Alsace Gewürztraminer, or an aged Coteaux du Layon Chenin Blanc! At the end of the day it's all pretty subjective.

So what follows is only my own broad guidelines for matching wines to the main dish of the meal, or to special types of meals, such as barbecues, take-aways and picnics. I hope that the ideas will serve as a starting point for anyone who wants to widen the range of wines which they serve at home and that it will encourage lots of experimentation and discussion!

Food and wine partnerships

In no particular order:

TAKE-AWAY MEALS

Chinese: Red wines are not brilliant with Chinese food though I think you can just about get away with Beaujolais or a red wine from the Loire such as Chinon or Saumur Champigny. Rosé is better. There's a reason why Mateus is so popular in Asian restaurants and that's that it tastes good with the food! Anjou Rosé is not so good. For white wine, try any Riesling wine: dry from Alsace, medium dry from Germany. Australian Rhine Riesling works well with rich sauces and German halbtrocken wines with deep fried food and dim sum. Claret is surprisingly good with Peking duck, but go easy on the hoisin sauce.

Indian: The wine nearly always comes off second best here, so a fresh and light red or white will probably do. Listel Gris is good with curried fish and Gewürztraminer with tandoori dishes. Australian Shiraz may also take the curry head on. Otherwise, stick to simple Eastern European Cabernet Sauvignon or Beaujolais.

Mexican: All that chilli is even more of a problem. Stick to wines in the light and fresh categories. You could also drink up wines which you have found to be too astringent. The chilli seems to kill the acidity and what fruit there is in the wine comes through!

Fish and chips: Fresh light wines with good acidity are needed to cut through the rich batter. Try white Vins de Pays wines, Muscadet or Pinot Grigio or if you like a stronger flavour, one of the Sauvignon wines from Hungary, the Czech Republic, the Loire or Bordeaux (see also Fishy Feasts). For something a touch sweeter try the Bulgarian Country whites.

Pizza-to-go: For the reds, choose from the light or medium-bodied Vin de Pays from southern France, Chianti or Rosso di Montalcino. Try one of the fuller-flavoured whites from the new world to match the tomato and herbs or a dry Italian white from the Veneto or Trentino to cope with rich toppings.

Hamburgers: Good straightforward Bulgarian Cabernet Sauvignon is an excellent choice here. Or if you want to splash out a bit more try an Australian Cabernet Sauvignon.

Barbecues: If it's to be a barbecue party, go for one of the party wines listed. Fresh and light Vin de Pays and Eastern European reds work well too. If it's a more serious meal, then choose from the medium-bodied reds for plain grills and from the fuller-flavoured reds and whites for marinated and basted dishes. Favourites are Chianti with herby sausages, Chilean Merlot with spicy drumsticks and Australian Cabernet/Shiraz with barbecued spare-ribs.

ROAST DINNERS

Meat: Simple roast beef, lamb and pork all show off good wines. Claret is traditional with roast beef, but any of the wines in the medium-bodied red section or full-flavoured whites should be good. Lamb needs something a little lighter so try a Beaujolais, Zinfandel or a red wine like Chinon from the Loire Valley.

Chicken: Almost any wine works well with roast chicken, though those in the fuller-bodied red section could be a bit overpowering.

Duck: Duck can be a bit fatty and so an element of acidity is needed. The tannin in red wine does not go well with duck, so try a fruity wine such as Beaujolais, Zinfandel or a light red Vin de Pays. White wines from the Loire, like Vouvray, are good with duck or for something rather different try an oaky New World Chardonnay.

Game: This is always rich meat and the fuller-bodied flavoured wines are best. Try Syrah-based wines from the Rhône or Shiraz from Australia, Rioja or one of the Portuguese wines, such as Bairrada or Alentejo. White wine lovers should try a German Auslese medium dry wine.

CHRISTMAS DINNERS

Turkey: Like chicken, this meat is very easy to match. It will be the stuffing or the accompaniments which may swing the choice to or from a particular style. New World Chardonnay goes well with turkey, but claret is the classic choice.

Goose: This is not nearly as fatty when it is cooked as everyone seems to think, but it is well flavoured. Try Pinot Gris/Tokai or Gewürztraminer from Alsace, or an Auslese Riesling from Germany. Good reds include Fitou, full-bodied Côtes-du-Rhône or Australian Cabernet Shiraz.

FISHY FEASTS

The combination of red wine and white fish can leave a kind of metallic flavour in the mouth, though not everyone experiences this. This is worse with more tannic wines than with fresh and fruity ones. The lighter Vin de Pays, Beaujolais, Hungarian Merlot-based wines, Loire reds and Bardolino are all worth trying with well-flavoured fish like salmon, fried fish or fish stews and casseroles.

Most white wines in the fresh and light category will go well with fish and with shellfish. Don't forget the German trocken wines here. The fuller-flavoured Chardonnay-based wines will go well with fish in rich sauces.

POPULAR CLASSICS

Here are a few of the combinations I have found successful in the last year:

Beef bourguignon: Red Burgundy, Rousillon or Rioja Reserva.

Beef stroganoff: Barbera d'Asti, Bulgarian Cabernet Sauvignon or Australian Cabernet/Shiraz.

Chicken in a cream sauce: German Riesling Kabinett, Hungarian or Italian Chardonnay or Alsace Pinot Blanc.

Chicken Kiev: Touraine Sauvignon, Orvieto, or Vin de Pays des Côtes de Gascogne.

Chilli con carne: Bardolino, most red or white Vin de Pays or a Hungarian Cabernet Sauvignon.

Coq au vin: Chianti Classico, Fitou or Faugères, claret, Australian Semillon/Chardonnay.

Duck à l'orange: Beaujolais, Vouvray or a German Kabinett.

Moussaka: Bulgarian Cabernet Sauvignon or Chianti

Pasta with tomato, basil and ham sauce: Toreldego Rotaliano, Montepulciano d'Abruzzo, Zinfandel

Quiche: Vins de Pays des Côtes de Gascogne, Alsace Pinot Blanc, red Bergerac or a claret.

Shepherd's pie: Any red or white Vins de Pays or an Eastern European or Chilean Cabernet Sauvignon.

Steak au poivre: Red Bergerac, Minervois or a Chianti.

Satay with peanut sauce: Australian Cabernet Shiraz or a good but not too assertive Sauvignon Blanc from Bordeaux, Chile or the Loire.

Wiener schnitzel: Bardolino, Barbera d'Asti, Muscadet or Italian Chardonnay.

VEGETARIAN FOOD

At first glance, vegetarian food seems quite easy to match to wine and, with the exception of some very strongly flavoured ones (parsnips, asparagus and turnips), vegetables do not pose too much of a problem. But real vegetarian food is not just vegetables. There are sauces and flavour combinations which need to be taken into account and vegetarians will need to think about the wines to match their food in much the same way as meat-eaters. Try Montepulciano d'Abruzzo with vegetarian lasagne, Hungarian Chardonnay with tofu and mushroom kebabs and a light red Spanish wine such as La Mancha with tortilla.

CHEESE BOARD

Do you serve the cheese-board before or after the dessert? Sometimes a matter of national pride, sometimes a matter of habit, the answer may well determine the choice of wine.

If you have moved from the savoury main course through a sweet dessert to the cheese board, you won't want to go back to an unfortified red wine. It will taste very harsh and dry after the sweetness of the dessert. This way of ordering the meal prevailed at English dinner parties and port was an obvious choice and very good it is too, but there are alternatives. Sweet white wine can go very well with blue cheese. Try it for yourself if you don't believe me. Combinations to try include Première Côte de Bordeaux with Blue Brie, Dolcelatte with Ste Croix-du-Mont or Stilton with Sauternes or Barsac.

In France, the cheese is traditionally served after the main course and before the dessert. This makes sense to the thrifty French mind. You do not need to introduce another wine if you don't want to - simply go on drinking the red wine already on the table. Any adjustment can come in the choice of cheese to be served.

A mixed cheese board, so beloved of the dinner party hostess, is not a particularly good idea. Apart from the fact that you will inevitably be left with a fridge full of little bits of cheese for which you have no immediate use, you will also have to match the wine to the mildest cheese on the board.

Much better to serve one cheese which will really complement the wine you are drinking. This can be red or white. In fact, some cheese taste much better with white wine. Soft creamy cheeses, such as Brie and Camembert, are delicious with good Chardonnays (both Old and New World) and goat's cheese is good with Sauvignon.

Goat's cheese will also stand up to the tannin in heavier red wines, such as Châteauneuf-du-Pape, Rioja and some Australian reds. The tannin in these wines can be a problem with milder cow's milk cheese.

Light Vin de Pays wines, Beaujolais, Valpolicella and Bardolino are good choices for almost all cheeses. Another good idea is to choose wine and cheese from the same country or area. Ideas include Chianti with Pecorino, Hautes Côtes de Nuits with Cendre, or Barbaresco with Gorgonzola.

Best wine buys in the high street

Categories and keys

Wine can be drunk on many occasions. You may want to choose something to go with the Sunday roast or you might just want to enjoy a glass while sitting reading a newspaper in the garden. You may be planning a barbecue, a wine and cheese party, or a special anniversary dinner party. All of these occasions call for a different style of wine.

Of course, I have not been able to be quite so specific in the categories I have chosen to list the wines, but I hope that they will at least help you to check through the wine shelves more quickly.

Here is the thinking behind each category:

White wines

FRESH AND LIGHT WINES FOR EASY DRINKING AT ANY TIME

These are dry white wines which I might choose to drink at almost any time. They can be drunk on their own on a summer's day or during an evening of conversation or cards. They would make a good accompaniment to a light meal or you could serve them at a party. They are fresh but not sharp and they are usually quite uncomplicated. The Sauvignon wines probably have the most distinctive taste.

FULLER-FLAVOURED AND FRUITY, BUT STILL RELATIVELY DRY, WINES

These wines are rather more complex and have a very definite character of their own. This certainly does not preclude them being drunk alone, but they will stand up to quite definite food. Some of them, like the full-blown Australian wines, make excellent aperitifs - two glasses and you are ready for something less opulent. Yet others, such as the Australian Rhine Rieslings and some Vouvrays, have a higher degree of residual sugar but do not taste as sweet as, say, German wines so I have included in this section.

MEDIUM DRY, VERY FRUITY, WINES TO SERVE AT ANY TIME

The white wines in this category are medium dry in character. They may be quite light and flowery like the German choices or they may be heavier and more distinctive. They should not be cloying. Ideally their relative sweetness is balanced by good acidity so that you are left with a pleasant non-sweet taste in the mouth. Some of them make excellent aperitifs.

SPARKLING WINES FOR APERITIFS AND PARTIES

The prickle of bubbles adds a festive feel to wine. These wines are great for celebrations and anniversaries, but they do tend to cost rather more and so I have raised the ceiling in this category from £5.00 to £8.00.

DESSERT OR PUDDING WINES

These are sweet wines to serve at the end of the meal. Like the medium dry wines they should have good balancing acidity plus a good depth of flavour.

GOOD WINES FOR PARTIES

These wines are chosen both for their easy-drinking qualities and for their value. The wine you serve at a party should not be boring, but nor should it be too distinctive. If it is, some guests may not like it at all and others may not want to drink more than a couple of glasses of it. After all, not everyone likes heavily oaked white wines or very tannic reds.

SPLASHING OUT

There are some occasions when you may want to spend more than my self-imposed £5.00 limit. These represent just a few of the fine wines I have tasted in the high street.

Red wines

LIGHT AND FRUIT WINES FOR EASY DRINKING AT ANY TIME

The red wines in this section correspond to the Fresh and Light category in the white wine section. The wines are good to drink on their own but they may also quite happily be drunk with simple, everyday meals.

MEDIUM-BODIED WINES TO SERVE ON THEIR OWN OR WITH FOOD

The red wines in this category are not sweet, rather they are wines which I find to be particularly versatile. They will partner all kinds of food, but can also be served at parties or be drunk by the glass on a quiet evening at home.

HEAVIER WINES TO SERVE WITH FOOD

As the title suggests, these wines are probably heavier in alcohol (though not always) and are likely to be more distinctive in flavour, perhaps with some oak about the place. They can usually be served with well-flavoured food and indeed may be improved by the match.

GOOD WINES FOR PARTIES and SPLASHING OUT

The same criteria apply here as for white wines.

Descriptions

I hope that these categories give a useful indication of the style of wine to expect. Where a wine is particularly fruity or oaky or has a distinctive flavour all its own I have indicated this in the lists. I have also singled out wines which are particularly easy to drink.

I have deliberately avoided longer descriptions because I feel that descriptive words such as 'fruity' are bound to crop up for many of the wines thus rendering the description meaningless. After all I would not have chosen to list the wine if I did not feel it had the qualities of a reasonable wine.

More specific descriptive words such as those outlined on pages 9–10 may not mean the same thing to my readers as they do to me and so I have decided not to change the nature of the book in this way.

I have, however, rather reluctantly decided to list under their own side headings those wines which feature the extremely popular Chardonnay, Sauvignon Blanc or Cabernet Sauvignon grape varieties. My reluctance stems from the fact that I would be very sad it this meant that some really interesting wines not made from these grape varieties were neglected.

* The stars given to some wines reflect my opinion that they are particularly good wines in their price range.

Wine Development Board taste guides

In addition to the headings outlined above, I have also included the ratings from the Wine Development Board (now wound up) guide to sweetness and dryness. This guide is accepted by the EU and you may find the symbols (see page 34) used either on the supermarket shelves or on the bottle label itself.

The guide is intended to help new wine-drinkers to find their way around the most important part of the taste characteristics of white wine - the sweetness. The guide uses a scale from 1 to 9. Starting at 1, the wines are bone dry and may be quite sharp and fresh. At 9, at the other end of the scale, are the really sweet wines.

In the middle of the scale, around 3 and 4, the acidity levels of the wine may mask the sweetness. Vinho Verde, for example, is a wine which tastes much dryer than it really is. Other wines do not seem so sweet because they are so full of rich fruit flavours. Australian Chenin Blanc and Rhine Riesling fall into this category.

The Board also developed a red wine guide which is not very widely accepted and which can be very confusing. Accordingly I have decided not to use it in my listing this year. However, a few outlets still use it with their shelf descriptions and so I have set out the symbols below.

It uses a simple five-point alphabetical scale. The categories attempt to identify red wine in terms of total taste or the impression that they make on the palate. Starting at A, the wines are undemanding and very easy to drink. At E, at the other end of the scale, they are bigger and have more concentrated styles. The wines here give a greater sensation of depth and fullness in the mouth.

Bergerac
Chablis
Champagne
Dry White Bordeaux
Entre-Deux-Mers
Manzanilla Sherry
Muscadet
Pouilly Blanc Fumé
Sancerre
Saumur
Tavel Rosé
Touraine

Allela
Chardonnay from all countries
Dry English wine
Dry Montilla
Dry Sherry
Dry Sparkling wine (Brut)
Dry Vouvray
Fendant
Fino Sherry
Frascati Secco
German Trocken wines
Graves
La Mancha
Navarra
Orvieto

Pale Dry Cyprus Sherry
Penedès
Riesling d'Alsace
Rueda
Sercial Madeira
Spanish Dry White
Soave
Valencia
Verdicchio
White Burgundy
White Rhône

Brut Sparkling wine
Dry Amontillado Sherry
Dry White Vermouth
Grüner Veltliner Austrian
Halbtrocken German wines
Hungarian Olasz Rizling Dry
Medium Dry English
Medium Dry Montilla
Medium Dry Vermouth
Moseltaler
Muscat d'Alsace
Pinot Blanc d'Alsace

Golden Sherry
Demi-Sec Sparkling and Demi-Sec Champange
German Spätlesen
Tokay Szamarodni Sweet

Anjou Rosé
Australian and New Zealand Rhine Riesling
Bulgarian Olasz Rizling
Chenin Blanc
Full Amontillado
German Kabinett
German Quality wine (Qba)
Gewürztraminer d'Alsace
Hungarian Olasz Rizling Medium Dry
Medium Dry English
Medium Dry Montilla
Medium Dry Sherry
Medium Dry Vermouth
Orvieto Abboccato
Other Gewürztraminers
Portuguese Rosé
Vinho Verde
Yugoslav Laski Rizling

Asti Spumante
Rosso, Rosé and Bianco Vermouth
Bual Madeira
German Auslesen
Monbazillac
Montilla Cream
Pale Cream Sherry
Premières Côtes de Bordeaux
Today Aszu
White Port

Barsac
Cream Cyprus Sherry
Cream Sherry
Dark Cream and Rich Cream Sherry
German and Austrian Beerenauslesen
German Eiswein
Moscatels/Muscats
Sauternes
Spanish Sweet White

Austrian Spätlese
Dry White Port
EEC Table Wine
Liebfraumilch
Medium Cyprus Sherry
Verdelho Madeira
Vouvray Demi-Sec

Brown Sherry
German and Austrian Trockenbeerenauslesen
Malaga
Malmsey Madeira
Marsala
Muscat de Beaumes de Venise

Bardolino
Beaujolais
EEC Table wines
German Red
Touraine
Vin de Table
Vino da Tavola

Beaujolais Villages and Crus
Chinon
Côtes du Roussillon
Merlot from all countries
Navarra
Pinot Noir from all countries
Red Burgundy
Saumur
Valdepeñas
Valencia
Valpolicella
Vin de Pays

Bergerac
Bordeaux Rouge/Claret
Bulgarian Cabernet Sauvignon
Corbières
Côtes-du-Rhône
Minervois
North African Red
Rioja

Bairrada
Cabernet Sauvignon from all countries
except Bulgaria
Châteauneuf-du-Pape
Chianti
Crozes-Hermitage
Dão
Fitou
Hungarian Red
Médoc
Penedés
Ribera del Duero
Rioja Reserves
Ruby and Tawny Port

Barolo
Cyprus Red
Greek Red
Jumilla
Recioto della Valpolicella
Shiraz from Australia and South Africa

Keys for the wines' country of origin

AR	=	Argentina	H	=	Hungary
0Z	=	Australia	IT	=	Italy
A	=	Austria	MAC	=	Macedonia
BR	=	Brazil	MO	=	Moldavia
BU	=	Bulgaria	NZ	=	New Zealand
CH	=	Chile	P	=	Portugal
CR	=	Croatia	R	=	Romania
CZ	=	Czech Republic	SA	=	South Africa
E	=	England	SL	=	Slovakia
EU	=	Europe	SP	=	Spain
FR	=	France	USA	=	United States of America
GER	=	Germany			

*	=	Wines which are particularly good in their price range
VdP	=	Vin de Pays

WHITE

- *Fresh and light wines for easy drinking at any time*

Asda Sicilian Bianco	IT	②	£2.50-3.00
Asda Vino da Tavola Bianco	IT	②	£2.50-3.00
Asda Hungarian Pinot Blanc	HU	②	£2.50-3.00
Chenin VdP de la Haute Vallée de l'Aude	FR	②	£3.00-3.50*
Asda Frascati Superiore *(distinctive)*	IT	②	£3.00-3.50
Asda Dry Vinho Verde	P	③	£3.00-3.50
Château Fondarzac Entre-deux-Mers	FR	②	£3.50-4.00
Orvieto Classico Secco Cardeto	IT	②	£3.50-4.00
Soave Classico Corte Olive Lenotti *(particularly fruity)*	IT	②	£3.50-4.00*
Pinot Grigio Ca Pradai Bidoli	IT	②	£3.50-4.00
Muscadet de Sèvre-et-Maine Sur Lie Domain Guy Bossard *(organic)*	FR	②	£4.50-5.00*

Sauvignon Blanc and Sauvignon-based wines

Domaine St Francois Sauvignon VdP d'Oc	FR	①	£3.00-3.50*
Asda Côtes de Duras Sauvignon	FR	①	£3.00-3.50
Van Loveren Robertson Sauvignon Blanc *(particularly fruity)*	SA	①	£3.50-4.00
Asda Sauvignon Blanc	CH	①	£3.50-4.00

- *Fuller-flavoured and fruity, but still relatively dry, wines*

Asda Hungarian Muscat *(distinctively fruity)*	HU	②	£2.50-3.00*
Clearsprings Cape White	SA	②	£2.50-3.00
Fairview Estate Gewürztraminer *(distinctive)*	USA	②	£4.00-4.50

36

Hill Smith Old Triangle Riesling	OZ	④	£4.00-4.50
Barramundi Semillon South Eastern	OZ	②	£4.00-4.50

Chardonnay and Chardonnay blends

Preslav Chardonnay/Sauvignon Vintage Blend *(distinctive)*	HU	②	£2.50-3.00
Hungarian Chardonnay Private Reserve Mecsekalji *(particularly fruity)*	HU	②	£3.00-3.50
Asda SE Australia Semillon/ Chardonnay *(particularly fruity)*	OZ	②	£3.00-3.50*
Asda Chilean Chardonnay	CH	②	£3.50-4.00
Van Loveren Spe Bona Chardonnay Reserve *(particularly fruity)*	SA	②	£4.00-4.50*
Asda South Australia Chardonnay	OZ	②	£4.00-4.50*
Rowan Brook Chardonnay Reserve *(oaky)*	CH	②	£4.50-5.00*

• *Medium dry, very fruity, wines to serve at any time*

Asda Niersteiner Spiegelberg Kabinett	GER	④	£3.00-3.50*
Asda Wiltinger Scharzberg Riesling Kabinett	GER	④	£3.00-3.50
Asda Mainzer Domherr Spätlese	GER	④	£3.00-3.50

• *Sparkling wines for aperitifs and parties*

Asda Asti	IT	⑦	£4.50-5.00*
River Run Export Brut Reserve	OZ	②	£4.50-5.00*
Varichon et Clerc Sparkliing Chardonnay	FR	②	£5.00-5.50*
Asda Cava	SP	①	£5.00-5.50*
Marquès de Monistrol	SP	①	£6.00-6.50

• *Dessert or pudding wines*

Asda Moscatel de Valencia	SP	⑨	£2.50-3.00*
Muscat Cuvée Henry Peyrottes	FR	⑦	£3.50-4.00*

Château Mouney Premières Côtes de Bordeaux	FR	⑦	£4.00-4.50

- ### *Good wines for parties*
Le Pigoulet VdP des Gers *(easy drinking)*	FR	②	£2.50-3.00
Asda Hungarian Chardonnay	HU	②	£2.50-3.00
Asda Cape White *(easy drinking)*	SA	②	£2.50-3.00
VdP des Côtes de Gascogne	FR	②	£3.00-3.50

- ### *Splashing out*
Goundrey Langton Chardonnay *(particularly fruity)*	OZ	②	£5.00-5.50
Mitchelton Marsanne *(distinctive)*	OZ	②	£5.00-5.50*
Graacher Himmelreich Riesling Kabinett	GER	④	£6.00-6.50*

RED AND ROSÉ

- ### *Light and fruity wines for easy drinking at any time*
Riva Sangiovese di Romagna *(easy drinking)*	IT	£2.50-3.00
Asda Merlot Villany	HU	£2.50-3.00
Kekfrankos Villany	HU	£2.50-3.00*
Asda Beajolais *(easy drinking)*	FR	£3.00-3.50
Domaine de Barjac VdP du Gard *(particularly fruity) (organic)*	FR	£3.00-3.50
Romanian Pinot Noir	RO	£3.00-3.50*
Santa Helena Chilean Rosé *(particularly fruity)*	CH	£3.00-3.50*
Asda Sangiovese delle Marche	IT	£3.00-3.50
Pinot Noir VdP de l'Aude *(oaky)*	FR	£3.50-4.00

Fairview Estate Dry Rosé
(*particularly fruity*)   USA   £3.50-4.00

- *Medium-bodied wines to serve on their own or with food*

Asda Corbières	FR	£2.50-3.00
Asda Sicilian Rosso	IT	£2.50-3.00
Don Darias *(oaky)*	SP	£2.50-3.00
Asda Fitou	FR	£3.00-3.50
Asda Douro *(particularly fruity)*	P	£3.00-3.50*
Caramany Côtes du Rousillon Villages	FR	£3.50-4.00*
Château la Ramière Côtes-du-Rhône *(distinctive)*	FR	£3.50-4.00*
Chianti Salvanza Colli Senesi *(particularly fruity)*	IT	£3.50-4.00*
Mas Segala Côtes du Roussillon Villages	FR	£4.00-4.50*
Barbera d'Asti Cantine Gemma	IT	£4.50-5.00*
Fairview Estate Shiraz	SA	£4.50-5.00*

Cabernet Sauvignon and Cabernet blends

Asda Cabernet Sauvignon VdP d'Oc *(easy drinking and fruity)*	FR	£2.50-3.00*
Asda Hungarian Cabernet Sauvignon *(particularly easy drinking and fruity)*	HU	£2.50-3.00*
Asda Claret *(particularly fruity)*	FR	£3.00-3.50*
Château Haut-Saric Bordeaux	FR	£3.00-3.50*
Oriachovitza Cabernet Sauvignon Reserve *(distinctive)*	BU	£3.00-3.50*
Rowanbrook Chilean Cabernet/ Malbec *(particularly fruity)*	CH	£3.00-3.50
Asda South Eastern Australia Shiraz/ Cabernet *(easy-drinking)*	OZ	£3.00-3.50

- *Heavier wines to serve with food*

Asda Cahors	FR	£3.00-3.50

| Asda Fitou | FR | £3.00-3.50 |

Cabernet Sauvignon and Cabernet blends

Asda Chilean Cabernet/Merlot	CH	£3.50-4.00
Hardy's Nottage Hill Cabernet Sauvignon	OZ	£4.00-4.50
Berri Estates Cabernet/Shiraz	OZ	£4.00-4.50

• *Good wines for parties*

Asda VdP de l'Aude	FR	£2.50-3.00
Asda Merlot VdP d'Oc	FR	£2.50-3.00
Asda St Chinon *(easy drinking)*	FR	£2.50-3.00

• *Splashing out*

Asda Red Burgundy	FR	£5.00-5.50
Chianti Classico Quercia al Poggio	IT	£5.00-5.50*
Rioja Crainza Campillo	SP	£5.00-5.50*
Rowanbrook Reserve Cabernet Sauvignon *(particularly fruity)*	CH	£5.00-5.50*

Augustus Barnett

This chain of off-licences has been taken over by the Victoria Wine Company and all stores will become either Victoria Wine Cellars or Victoria Wine Shops. See page 115 for the Victoria Wine Company list.

Bottoms Up

This chain of high street off-licences is now part of the Thresher Group and many of the same wines are stocked in both stores, though Bottoms Up does stock some additional wines. However, because of the size of the overlap I have listed all my recommendations for both stores under Thresher on page 107.

Budgens

WHITE

- *Fresh and light wines for easy drinking at any time*

Budgens Muscadet	FR	①	£3.00-3.50
Gaillac Blanc	FR	②	£3.50-4.00
Tuileries du Bosc VdP de St-Mont	FR	②	£3.50-4.00*
Château Megyer Tokaji Furmint *(distinctive)*	HU	②	£4.00-4.50

Sauvignon Blanc and Sauvignon-based wine

Domaine Villeroy-Castellas Sauvignon Blanc	FR	①	£3.50-4.00*

- *Fuller-flavoured and fruity, but still relatively dry, wines*

VdP Catalan des Pyrenees Orientales Muskat *(distinctively fruity)*	FR	②	£3.00-3.50
Hardy's RR *(particularly fruity)*	OZ	②	£4.00-4.50
Pinot Blanc d'Alsace Gisselbrecht	FR	②	£4.50-5.00 *

41

Chardonnay and Chardonnay blends

Hungarian Chardonnay	HU	②	£3.00-3.50
Jacob's Creek Semillon/			
Chardonnay	OZ	②	£4.00-4.50
Glen Ellen Proprietors Reserve			
Chardonnay (*particularly fruity*)	USA	②	£4.00-4.50*

- *Medium dry, very fruity, wines to serve at any time*

Bereich Bernkastel	GER	④	£2.50-3.00
Klüssrather St Michael Kabinett	GER	④	£3.00-3.50
Baden Gewürztraminer Reserve			
(*particularly fruity*)	GER	④	£4.50-5.00*

- *Sparkling wines for aperitifs and parties*

Flinders Creek Brut Rosé	OZ	②	£5.00-5.50*
Asti Martini	IT	⑦	£6.00-6.50
Martini Brut	IT	①	£6.00-6.50
Lindauer Brut	NZ	①	£7.00-7.50

- *Good wines for parties*

Tocai del Veneto Vina da Tavola			
Zonin (*easy drinking*)		②	£2.50-3.00
Domaine Bonnefois VdP de Côtes de			
Gascogne	FR	②	£3.00-3.50

- *Splashing out*

Château de la Jaubertie Bergerac	FR	①	£5.00-5.50*
Lugana Villa Flora	IT	②	£5.00-5.50*

RED AND ROSÉ

- *Light and fruity wines for easy drinking at any time*

Merlot del Veneto Vino da Tavola	IT		£2.50-3.00

Le Haut Colombier VdP de la			
Drome	FR		£3.00-3.50*
Budgens Valpolicella	IT		£3.00-3.50
Listel Gris de Gris Rosé	FR	②	£3.50-4.00
Dornfelder Neirsteiner			
Klostergarten *(easy drinking)*	GER		£3.50-4.00

• *Medium-bodied wines to serve on their own or with food*

Faugères Maison Jeanjean	FR	£3.00-3.50
Château Bassanel Minervois	FR	£3.50-4.00
Abbaye St Milaire Côteaux Varois	FR	£3.50-4.00*
Château de Malijay Côtes-du-Rhône	FR	£4.00-4.50*
Côtes de St Mont Tuilerie du Bosc	FR	£4.00-4.50
Brown Brothers Tarango		
(particularly fruity)	OZ	£4.50-5.00*

Cabernet Sauvignon and Cabernet blends

Cabernet Sauvignon Plovdiv Region	BU	£3.00-3.50
Hungarian Cabernet Sauvigon	HU	£3.00-3.50

• *Heavier wines to serve with food*

Marquès de Caro Reserva		
(distinctive)	SP	£3.00-3.50*
Viña Albali Valdepeñas	SP	£3.50-4.00
Jacob's Creek Dry Red	OZ	£4.00-4.50
Undurraga Cabernet Sauvignon	CH	£4.00-4.50

• *Good wine for parties*

VdP des Côteaux de l'Ardèche	FR	£2.50-3.00

Cellar 5

WHITE

- *Fresh and light wines for easy drinking at any time*
  | Muscadet de Sèvre-et-Maine | FR | ① | £3.50-4.00 |
  | Pinot Bianco Trentino | IT | ② | £3.50-4.00 |
  Sauvignon Blanc and Sauvignon-based wines
  | Cape Country Sauvignon Blanc | SA | ① | £3.00-3.50 |
  | Sauvignon de Touraine | FR | ① | £4.50-5.00 |

- *Fuller-flavoured and fruity, but still relatively dry, wines*
  | KWV Chenin Blanc | SA | ③ | £3.50-4.00 |
  Chardonnay and Chardonnay blends
Hungarian Chardonnay	HU	②	£2.50-3.00
Chardonnay Trentino	IT	②	£3.50-4.00
Coldridge Semillon/Chardonnay	OZ	②	£3.50-4.00*
Santa Carolina Chardonnay	CH	②	£4.50-5.00*

- *Medium dry, very fruity, wines to serve at any time*
Slaviantzi Muscat/Ugno Blanc	BU	④	£2.50-3.00
Bereich Bernkastel	GER	③	£3.0-3.50
Oppenheimer Krötenbrunnen	GER	⑤	£3.50-4.00

- *Sparkling wines for aperitifs and parties*
Moscato Lanza	IT	⑦	£3.50-4.00
Seppelts Great Western Brut	OZ	②	£4.50-5.00
Angas Brut	OZ	①	£5.50-6.00
Asti Martini	IT	⑦	£6.50-7.00
Lindauer Brut	OZ	①	£6.50-7.00

- *Dessert or pudding wine*
  | Coldridge Late Picked Muscat | OZ | ⑦ | £4.00-4.50 |

- *Good wine for parties*
  Cape Country White *(easy drinking)*   SA   ②   £3.00-3.50

- *Splashing out*
  Oxford Landing Chardonnay   OZ   £5.00-5.50
  Mitchelton Marsanne *(distinctive)*   OZ   £6.50-7.00

RED

- *Light and fruity wines for easy drinking at any time*

Hungarian Merlot	HU	£2.50-3.00
Côtes-du-Rhône	FR	£3.50-4.00
Bulgarian Merlot	BU	£3.00-3.50
Fortant Merlot VdP d'Oc	FR	£3.50-4.00

- *Medium-bodied wines to serve on their own or with food*

Corbières Château Mandrelle	FR	£3.00-3.50
Château Canet Minervois	FR	£3.00-3.50

  Cabernet Sauvignon and Cabernet blends

Hungarian Cabernet Sauvignon	HU	£2.50-3.00
Cabernet Sauvignon Fortant VdP	FR	£4.00-4.50
Santa Carolina Cabernet/Merlot	CH	£4.00-4.50
Santa Cabernet Sauvignon *(particularly fruity)*	CH	£4.50-5.00*

- *Heavier wines to serve with food*

Campo Viejo Crianza Rioja	SP	£4.50-5.00
Torres Sangredetoro	SP	£4.50-5.00

  Cabernet Sauvignon and Cabernet blends

Coldridge Shiraz/Cabinet	OZ	£3.50-4.00

- *Good wines for parties*

VdP Côtes de Gascogne Rouge	FR	£2.50-3.00

Cape Country Red *(easy drinking)*	SA	£3.00-3.50
Splashing out		
Campo Viejo Reserva Rioja	SP	£5.50-6.00

Co-op

A wide range of wines are bought centrally by the Co-operative Wholesale Society and this list is based on those purchases. You will find all the wines at CWS Retail stores.

The wines are also offered to the other retail societies and managers at each society decide which of the wines, if any, to buy. Thus you may find that your branch of the Co-op does not stock all of these wines.

WHITE

- *Fresh and light wines for easy drinking at any time*

Co-op Sicilian White *(easy drinking)*	IT	②	£2.50-3.00
Co-op VdP des Côtes du Gascogne	FR	①	£3.00-3.50
Co-op Muscadet	FR	①	£3.00-3.50
Co-op Baden Dry *(particularly fruity)*	GER	②	£3.00-3.50
Co-op Navarra Blanco	SP	②	£3.00-3.50
Co-op Bianco di Custoza	IT	②	£3.50-4.00
Muscadet de Sèvre-et-Maine Sur Lie	FR	①	£4.50-5.00

Sauvignon Blanc and Sauvignon blends

Touraine Sauvignon Domaine du			
Clos de Bourg	FR	①	£3.00-3.50
Château Pierrousselle Blanc			
(particularly fruity)	FR	①	£3.50-4.00*
Peteroa Sauvignon Blanc	CH	①	£3.50-4.00

- **Fuller-flavoured and fruity, but still relatively dry, wines**
    - Co-op Cape White *(easy drinking)*   SA   ③   £3.00-3.50
    - **Chardonnay and Chardonnay blends**
    - Co-op Chardonnay Atesino
        (particularly fruity)   IT   ②   £3.00-3.50
    - Co-op Jacaranda Hill Semillon/
        Chardonnay *(particularly fruity)*   ②   £3.00-3.50*
    - VdP d'Oc Chardonnay Fleur du
        Moulin   FR   ②   £3.50-4.00*

- **Medium dry, very fruity, wines to serve at any time**
    - Co-op Anjou Blanc   FR   ③   £3.00-3.50
    - Three Choirs New Release
        (particularly fruity)   E   ③   £3.00-3.50
    - Co-op Oppenheimer
        Krötenbrunnen   GER   ⑤   £3.00-3.50
    - St Ursula Galerie Riesling   GER   ④   £3.50-4.00

- **Sparkling wines for aperitifs and parties**
    - Co-op Sparkling Liebfraumilch   GER   ⑥   £4.00-4.50
    - Co-op Cava   SP   ②   £5.00-5.50
    - Co-op Sparkling Saumur
        (particularly fruity)   FR   ②   £6.50-7.00*

- **Dessert or pudding wines**
    - Co-op Spätlese Pfalz
        (distinctively fruity)   GER   ⑥   £3.50-4.00*
    - Monbazillac Domaine du Haut
        Rauly *(half)*   FR   ⑧   £3.50-4.00*

- **Good wines for parties**
    - Château Grand Pereau
        (easy drinking)   FR   ①   £2.50-3.00*
    - Co-op Hungarian White
        (particularly fruity)   HU   ③   £2.50-3.00
    - Co-op California Colombard   USA   ①   £3.00-3.50

- *Splashing out*

Co-op Alsace Gewürztraminer	FR	②	£5.50-6.00
Chablis Les Vignerons de Chablis	FR	①	£6.50-7.00*

RED

- *Light and fruity wines for easy drinking at any time*

Co-op VdP de l'Aude	FR	£2.50-3.00
Co-op Principato *(particularly fruity)*	IT	£2.50-3.00
Co-op Merlot and Kadarka	BU	£2.50-3.00
Co-op VdP d'Oc Cabernet Sauvignon	FR	£3.00-3.50*
Co-op Bergerac Rouge	FR	£3.00-3.50

- *Medium-bodied wines to serve on their own or with food*

Co-op Hungarian Red	HU	£2.50-3.00
Co-op Côtes-du-Rhône	FR	£3.00-3.50
Co-op Fitou	FR	£3.00-3.50
Co-op Navarra Tinto	SP	£3.00-3.50
Co-op Montepulciano d'Abruzzo *(distinctive)*	IT	£3.00-3.50
Co-op Cape Red *(easy drinking and fruity)*	SA	£3.00-3.50

  Cabernet Sauvignon and Cabernet blends

Co-op Bulgarian Cabernet Sauvignon	BU	£2.50-3.00
Co-op VdP d'Oc Cabernet Sauvignon	FR	£3.00-3.50
Co-op Cabernet Sauvignon Curico Valley	CH	£3.50-4.00*
Château Pierrouselle Bordeaux	FR	£4.00-4.50*

- *Heavier wines to serve with food*

Co-op Tempranillo *(oaky)*	SP	£ 2.50-3.00*
Co-op Bairrada Tinto	P	£3.00-3.50
Co-op Dao P *(distinctive)*		£3.00-3.50*

Cabernet Sauvignon and Cabernet blends

Co-op Jacaranda Hill Shiraz/ Cabernet *(particularly fruity)*	OZ	£3.00-3.50*
California Ruby Cabernet *(distinctive)*	USA	£3.00-3.50
Co-op Australian Cabernet Sauvignon	OZ	£4.00-4.50

- *Good wines for parties*

Co-op Sicilian Red	IT	£2.50-3.00
Co-op Côtes du Ventoux	FR	£3.00-3.50

- *Splashing out*

Vacqueyras Cuvée du Marquis de Fonseguille	FR	£5.50-6.00*

Davisons

WHITE

- *Fresh and light wines for easy drinking at any time*

Servus Burgenland *(easy drinking)*	A	③	£3.00-3.50
VdP des Côtes de Gascogne Cépage Colombard	FR	③	£3.50-4.00
Nuragus di Cagliari	IT	①	£3.50-4.00
Muscadet de Sèvre-et-Maine Pierre Millot	FR	①	£4.00-4.50
Bordeaux Sec	FR	①	£4.00-4.50

Frascati Secco Superiore Ambra	IT	②	£4.00-4.50
Torres Viña Sol	SP	①	£4.50-5.00

Sauvignon Blanc and Sauvignon blends

Sauvignon Blanc KWV	SA	①	£4.00-4.50

- *Fuller-flavoured and fruity, but still relatively dry, wines*

Muscat Ugni Blanc Country Wine			
(easy drinking)	BU	③	£2.50-3.00
Chenin Blanc KWV	SA	②	£4.00-4.50
Nobilo White Cloud Müller-Thurgau/			
Sauvignon Blanc	NZ	②	£4.00-4.50

Chardonnay and Chardonnay blends

Cape Cellars Chardonnay	SA	②	£3.50-4.00
Hardy's Stamp Series Semillon/			
Chardonnay	OZ	②	£3.50-4.00
Hardy's Nottage Hill Chardonnay	OZ	②	£4.00-4.50*
Jacob's Creek Semillon/			
Chardonnay	OZ	②	£4.00-4.50
Domaine de Pierre Jacques			
Chardonnay VdP d'Oc	FR	②	£4.50-5.00

- *Medium dry, very fruity, wines to serve at any time*

Piesporter Michelsberg	GER	③	£4.00-4.50
Niersteiner Gütes Domthal			
Huesgen	GER	③	£4.00-4.50
Gazela Vinho Verde	P	②	£4.00-4.50

- *Sparkling wines for aperitifs and parties*

Clair Diamant Blanc de Blanc Brut	FR	①	£5.00-5.50
Killawarra Brut	OZ	②	£5.50-6.00
Angas Brut	OZ	②	£6.00-6.50
Angas Brut Rosé	OZ	②	£6.00-6.50
Asti Martini	IT	⑤	£6.50-7.00
Ackerman Saumur Brut	FR	②	£7.00-7.50
Lindauer	NZ	②	£7.00-7.50

- *Dessert or pudding wine*
  Muscat Jose Sala   FR   ⑤   £4.00-4.50*

- *Good wines for parties*
  Chardonnay Sliven Region   BU   ②   £3.00-3.50
  Cape Cellars Sauvignon Blanc   SA   ①   £3.00-3.50

- *Splashing out*
  Cook's Chardonnay   NZ   ③   £5.00-5.50*
  Torres Viña Esmeralda   SP   ③   £5.50-6.00

RED

- *Light and fruity wines for easy drinking at any time*

Merlot del Veneto	IT	£3.00-3.50
Haskovo Merlot	BU	£3.00-3.50
Domaine de Pomaredes Merlot VdP d'Oc	FR	£3.50-4.00
Domaine de Limbardie VdP des Côteaux de Murviel	FR	£4.00-4.50

- *Medium-bodied wines to serve on their own or with food*

Toro Moralinos Tinto	SP	£3.00-3.50
Don Gulias Vino de Mesa	SP	£3.00-3.50
Côtes du Roussillon Villages	FR	£3.50-4.00
Minervois Domaine de St Eulalie	FR	£4.00-4.50
Pinotage KWV	SA	£4.00-4.50

Cabernet Sauvignon and Cabernet blends

Plovdiv Cabernet Sauvignon	BU	£3.50-4.00
Reserve Cabernet Sauvignon Russe	BU	£4.00-4.50
Bordeaux Rouge	FR	£4.00-4.50
Caliterra Cabernet Sauvignon	CH	£4.00-4.50

- **Heavier wines to serve with food**

Terras d'El Rei Tinto	P	£3.00-3.50
Penfold's Bin 2 Shiraz/Mataro	OZ	£4.50-5.00

Cabernet Sauvignon and Cabernet blends

Hardy's Stamp Series Shiraz/ Cabernet	OZ	£3.50-4.00
Hardy's Nottage Hill Cabernet Sauvignon	OZ	£4.00-4.50
Jacob's Creek Shiraz/Cabernet	OZ	£4.00-4.50

- **Good wines for parties**

Cabernet Sauvignon Minosegi Bor	HU	£2.50-3.00
Pavlikeni Cabernet/Merlot *(fruity and easy drinking)*	BU	£2.50-3.00

- **Splashing out**

Rocce Delle Macie Chianti Classico	IT	£5.00-5.50
Marquès de Caceres Rioja Tinto	SP	£5.00-5.50
Jamieson's Run Coonawarra	OZ	£7.50-8.00*

Fullers and Bunches

WHITE

- **Fresh and light wines for easy drinking at any time**

Le Gascony Côtes des Gascogne *(particularly fruity)*	FR	②	£3.00-3.50*
Rioja d'Avalos Viura	SP	②	£3.00-3.50
Hauts de Bergelle Côtes de St-Mont	FR	②	£3.50-4.00
Torres Viña Sol Penedès	SP	②	£4.50-5.00

Sauvignon Blanc and Sauvignon-based wines

Côtes de Duras Sauvignon Blanc			
Berticot *(easy drinking)*	FR	①	£3.50-4.00
La Serre Sauvignon Blanc VdP d'Oc	FR	①	£3.50-4.00*
Hawkes Bay Estates Sauvignon			
Blanc *(particularly fruity)*	OZ	①	£4.50-5.00*

- *Fuller-flavoured and fruity, but still relatively dry, wines*

JP Vinhos Branco *(disinctive)*	P	②	£2.50-3.00
Leeton Downs Semillon *(oaky)*	OZ	②	£3.50-4.00*
Hardy's 'RR' *(distinctively fruity)*	OZ	③	£4.00-4.50*

Chardonnay and Chardonnay blends

Khan Krum Chardonnay Reserve	BU	②	£3.50-4.00
Gyongyos Chardonnay	HU	②	£3.50-4.00
La Serre Chardonnay VdP d'Oc	FR	②	£4.00-4.50
Penfolds Bin 21 Semillon/			
Chardonnay *(particularly fruity)*	OZ	②	£4.00-4.50*
Hardy's Nottage Hill Chardonnay			
(particularly fruity)	OZ	②	£4.00-4.50*

- *Medium dry, very fruity, wines to serve at any time*

Muskat & Ugni Blanc Country			
Wine *(easy drinking)*	BU	③	£2.50-3.00
Munsterer Schlosskapelle Kabinett	GER	④	£4.00-4.50
Wiltinger Scharzberg Riesling			
Kabinett	GER	④	£4.50-5.00

- *Sparkling wines for aperitifs and parties*

Yalumba Killawarra Rosé	OZ	③	£5.00-5.50
Angas Brut Rosé	OZ	②	£6.00-6.50
Blanquette de Limoux	FR	②	£6.50-7.00
Cordoniu Brut Cava	SP	①	£6.50-7.00

- *Dessert or pudding wines*

Castillo di Liria Moscatel de			
Valencia *(distinctively fruity)*	SP	⑤	£3.50-4.00*

- **Good wines for parties**

Castillo de Liria Valencia	SP	②	£3.00-3.50
Baden Dry	GER	②	£3.50-4.00

- **Splashing out**

Nobilo Marlborough Sauvignon	NZ	①	£5.00-5.50
Wirra Wirra Chardonnay			
(*oaky and fruity*)	OZ	②	£8.50-9.00*
Hunters Sauvignon	OZ	①	£9.00-9.50*

RED

- **Light and fruity wines for easy drinking at any time**

Suhindol Merlot	BU	£2.50-3.00
VdP de l'Aude de Cazes		
(*particularly fruity*)	FR	£2.50-3.00*
Domaine de St Laurent	FR	£2.50-3.00
Grenache Fortant de France		
VdP d'Oc (*particularly fruity*)	FR	£3.50-4.00*
Montepulciano d'Abruzzo Citra		
(*particularly fruity*)	IT	£3.50-4.00*
Teroldego Rotaliano		
(*particularly fruity*)	IT	£3.50-4.00

- **Medium-bodied wines to serve on their own or with food**

Rioja Casa del Marquès Sin Crianza	SP	£3.00-3.50
Suhindol Merlot Domaine Boyar		
(*particularly fruity*)	BU	£3.00-3.50*
Cuvée des Templiers VdP de		
Vaucluse (*particularly fruity*)	FR	£3.50-4.00
Rioja d'Avalos Tempranillo	SP	£3.50-4.00
Leetons Downs Shiraz/Grenache	OZ	£3.50-4.00

Domaine du Coudogno Faugères		
(easy drinking)	FR	£4.00-4.50*
Hauts de Bergelle Côtes de St-Mont	FR	£4.00-4.50*
Villa Bellafonte Chianti		
(particularly fruity)	IT	£4.00-4.50*
Château de Paraza Minervois		
Cuvée Speciale	FR	£4.50-5.00

Cabernet Sauvignon or Cabernet blends

Château Mayne de Baron Bordeaux	FR	£3.50-4.00*
Oriachovitza Cabernet Sauvignon		
Reserve	BU	£3.50-4.00*

- _**Heavier wines to serve with food**_

Torconal Merlot	CH	£3.50-4.00
Domaine Comte de Morgon		
VdP Côtes de Thongue	FR	£4.00-4.50
Gran Feudo Crianza Navarra		
(distinctive)		£4.00-4.50*
Faustino Rivero Ulecia Rioja	SP	£4.00-4.50*
Penfolds Bin 35 Cabernet/Shiraz		
(particularly fruity)	OZ	£4.50-5.00*
Torres Coronas Penedès	SP	£4.50-5.00*

- _**Good wines for parties**_

Castillo de Liria Red Navarra		
(easy drinking)	SP	£3.00-3.50
Rene Barbier Mediterranean Red	SP	£3.00-3.50

- _**Splashing out**_

Château Roquenagade Corbières		
(particularly fruity)	FR	£5.00-5.50*
Berri Estates Cabernet/Shiraz	OZ	£5.00-5.50*

Gateway

These stores are owned by Somerfield Stores Limited and as they are modernised they will be changing their names to Somerfield. For details of their wines see the entry for Somerfield on page 93.

House of Townend

WHITE

- *Fresh and light wines for easy drinking at any time*
  Colombard VdP des Côtes des
  Gascogne   FR ②   £3.50-4.00
  Côte du St Mont   FR ②   £3.50-4.00
  Domaine de Rieux VdP de Côtes
  de Gascogne *(particularly fruity)*   FR ①   £4.00-4.50*
  Côtes-du-Rhône Blanc Cellier des
  Dauphins   FR ②   £4.00-4.50
  Sauvignon Blanc and Sauvignon blends
  Portal del Alto Sauvignon Blanc   CH ①   £4.00-4.50
  Sutter Home Sauvignon   USA ①   £4.50-5.00

- *Fuller-flavoured and fruity, but still relatively dry, wines*
  Chardonnay and Chardonnay blends
  Pinot Chardonnay del Veneto Zonin IT ②   £3.50-4.00

Rowlands Brook Semillon/			
Chardonnay	OZ	②	£4.00-4.50*
Jacob's Creek Semillon			
Chardonnay	OZ	②	£4.00-4.50

- **_Medium dry, very fruity, wines to serve at any time_**

Niersteiner Gütes Domthal	GER	④	£3.00-3.50
Kreuzenacher Kronenburg	GER	④	£4.50-5.00
Slaviantsi Muscat and Ugni			
Blanc *(easy drinking)*	BU	④	£3.00-3.50
Russe Welschriesling	BU	④	£3.00-3.50*

- **_Sparkling wines for aperitifs and parties_**

Sparkling Liebfraumilch	GER	⑤	£4.50-5.00
Rowlands Brook Brut	OZ	②	£5.00-5.50
Asti Martini	IT	⑦	£6.50-7.00
Cordon Negro Brut	SP	②	£7.00-7.50
Diane de Poitiers Brut Chardonnay	FR	②	£7.50-8.00

- **_Good wines for parties_**

VdP de Vallée de Paradis	FR	②	£3.00-3.50
Pinot Grigio del Veneto	IT	①	£3.00-3.50

- **_Splashing out_**

Chardonnay Domaines Virginie			
VdP d'Oc	FR	②	£5.00-5.50*
Sauvignon de Haut Poitou	FR	①	£5.00-5.50
Penfolds Semillon/Chardonnay	OZ	②	£6.00-6.50

RED

- **_Light and fruity wines for easy drinking at any time_**

Haskova Merlot	BU		£3.00-3.50

Côtes du Luberon Rouge	FR	£3.50-4.00
Merlot Resplanday VdP d'Oc		
(particularly fruity)	FR	£3.50-4.00

- *Medium-bodied wines to serve on their own or with food*

Côtes du Roussillon de Mare	FR	£3.50-4.00
Château de Montrabech Corbières		
(easy drinking)	FR	£3.50-4.00
Côte du St Mont	FR	£3.50-4.00
Montepulciano d'Abruzzo		
(easy drinking)	IT	£3.50-4.00
Domaine de St Eulalie Minervois	FR	£4.00-4.50
Côtes-du-Rhône Cellier des		
Dauphins	FR	£4.00-4.50
Fitou Les Contemporains		
(particularly full and fruity)	FR	£4.50-5.00

Cabernet Sauvignon and Cabernet blends

Bulgarian Cabernet Sauvignon		
Svischtov	BU	£3.00-3.50
Russe Reserve Cabernet Sauvignon	BU	£4.00-4.50*

- *Heavier wines to serve with food*

Koonunga Hill Shiraz/Cabernet		
Penfolds	OZ	£3.00-3.50
Rowlands Brook Shiraz/Cabernet		
Penfolds	OZ	£4.00-4.50

- *Good wines for parties*

Les Vignerons Val d'Orbieu VdP		
Vallée du Paradis	FR	£3.00-3.50
Pavlikeni Cabernet/Merlot	BU	£3.00-3.50

- *Splashing out*

Bodegas Lanred Crianza Rioja	SP	£5.00-5.50*
Cuvée Privee Cellier des Dauphins		
(oaky)	FR	£6.00-6.50
Château Caronne Ste Gemme Haut		
Médoc	FR	£8.50-9.00

Leo's

This is the chain operated by Co-operative Retail Services, the largest of the retail co-operative societies. This list contains some Co-op wines but offers a larger percentage of its own purchases. These wines may also be found in Pioneer Stores.

WHITE

- *Fresh and light wines for easy drinking at any time*

Co-op Musacdet	FR	①	£2.50-3.00
Côtes de Duras	FR	②	£3.00-3.50
Co-op VdP des Côtes de Gascogne	FR	②	£3.00-3.50
Grave del Fruili Pinot Grigio	IT	②	£3.50-4.00

- *Fuller-flavoured and fruity, but still relatively dry, wines*

Muscat VdP des Pyrenees Orientales (*distinctively fruity*)	FR	③	£3.00-3.50
Baden Dry	GER	②	£3.50-4.00
Coldridge Estate Semillon/ Chardonnay	OZ	②	£3.50-4.00
Co-op Alsace Pinot Blanc	FR	②	£4.50-5.00

Chardonnay and Chardonnay blends

Hungarian Chardonnay	HU	①	£2.50-3.00
Atesino Chardonnay (*particularly fruity*)	IT		£3.00-3.50
Ca Donini Chardonnay	IT	②	£3.50-4.00
Hardy's Stamp Series Semillon/ Chardonnay	OZ		£3.50-4.00
Hardy's Nottage Hill Chardonnay (*particularly fruity*)	OZ	②	£4.00-4.50*

- **Medium dry, very fruity, wines to serve at any time**

Binger St Rochuskapelle Spätlese	GER	⑤	£2.50-3.00
Leiwener Klöstergarten Riesling Kabinett	GER	④	£2.50-3.00

- **Sparkling wines for aperitifs and parties**

Seaview Brut	OZ	②	£5.50-6.00
Asti Martini	IT	⑤	£6.00-6.50
Condorniu Cava	SP	②	£6.50-7.00
Lindauer Brut	NZ	②	£7.00-7.50
Grandin Brut	FR	②	£7.50-8.00

- **Good wines for parties**

VdP de l'Aude	FR	②	£2.50-3.00
Castillo de Liria Valencia	SP	②	£3.00-3.50

- **Splashing out**

Rosémount Estate Chardonnay	OZ	②	6.00-6.50*

RED

- **Light and fruity wines for easy drinking at any time**

Hungarian Merlot	HU	£2.00-2.50
Co-op Principato *(particularly fruity)*	IT	£2.50-3.00
Classic Romanian Pinot Noir	RO	£2.50-3.00*
Co-op Bergerac Rouge	FR	£3.00-3.50

- **Medium-bodied wines to serve on their own or with food**

Co-op Navarra Tinto	SP	£2.50-3.00
Château du Bosc Coteaux du Languedoc *(particularly fruity)*	FR	£3.00-3.50*
Co-op Côtes-du-Rhône	FR	£3.00-3.40
Domaine de Barjac VdP du Gard *(organic)*	FR	£3.00-3.50

Celliers des Dauphins		
Côtes-du-Rhône	FR	£3.00-3.50
Valdezaro Chilean Red	CH	£3.00-3.50
Co-op Côtes de Provence Rouge	FR	£3.50-4.00
Montepulciano d'Abruzzo	IT	£3.50-4.00

Cabernet Sauvignon and Cabernet blends

Country Wine Cabernet/Merlot Pavlikeni	BU	£2.50-3.00
Hungarian Cabernet Sauvignon	BU	£2.50-3.00
Cabernet Sauvignon VdP d'Oc	FR	£3.00-3.50
Co-op Curico Valley Cabernet Sauvignon *(particularly fruity)*	CH	£3.50-4.00*

• *Heavier wines to serve with food*

Co-op Dão *(distinctive)*	P	£3.00-3.50*
Co-op Bairrada	P	£3.00-3.50
Viña Albali Valdepeñas	SP	£3.00-3.50
Jacob's Creek Dry Red	OZ	£3.50-4.00
Torres Coronas	SP	£4.50-5.00

Cabernet Sauvignon and Cabernet blends

Hungarian Cabernet Sauvignon	HU	£2.50-3.00
Coldridge Estate Shiraz/Cabernet	OZ	£3.50-4.00
Hardy's Nottage Hill Cabernet Sauvignon *(particularly fruity)*	OZ	£4.00-4.50*

• *Good wines for parties*

Castillo de Liria *(easy drinking)*	SP	£2.50-3.00
Blossom Hill Red	USA	£3.50-4.00

LiquorSave

LiquorSave is the alcoholic arm of Kwik Save. The wine buyers at this store have been working hard to find interesting wines at very reasonable prices. Last year they said that they hoped to have an even better range of wines this year and they have succeeded.

WHITE

- *Fresh and light wines for easy drinking at any time*

Comtesse de Lorancy	EU	②	£2.00-2.50
Gabbia d'Oro *(distinctive)*	IT	②	£2.00-2.50
Blanc de Blanc VdP des Côtes de Gascogne *(particularly fruity)*	FR	②	£2.50-3.00*
Côtes de Ventoux	FR	②	£2.50-3.00
Muscadet AC	FR	①	£2.50-3.00
Hungarian Chardonnay	HU	②	£2.50-3.00
Frascati *(particularly fruity)*	IT	①	£3.00-3.50
Blanc VdP de l'Hérault *(litre)*	FR	②	£3.00-3.50

Sauvignon Blanc or Sauvignon blends

Bordeaux Sauvignon Cuvée VE *(particularly fruity)*	FR	①	£2.50-3.00*

- *Fuller-flavoured and fruity, but still relatively dry, wines*

Pelican Bay Semillon South Australia	OZ	②	£2.50-3.00*

Chardonnay or Chardonnay blends

Steep Ridge Chardonnay/ Sauvignon VdP d'Oc *(distinctive)*	FR	①	£2.50-3.00
Hungarian Chardonnay	HU	②	£2.50-3.00
Angoves's Australian Chardonnay *(oaky)*	OZ	②	£3.50-4.00*

- *Medium dry, very fruity, wines to serve at any time*
  | Piesporter Michelsberg | GER | ⑤ | £2.50-3.00 |
  | Clearsprings Cape White | SA | ④ | £2.50-3.00 |

- *Sparkling wines for aperitifs and parties*
Sparkling Liebfraumilch	GER	④	£3.50-4.00
Asti Calvina	IT	⑦	£3.50-4.00
Asti Martini	IT	⑦	£5.50-6.00

- *Dessert and pudding wine*
  | Castillo de Liria Moscatel | | | |
  | *(distinctively fruity)* | SP | ⑨ | £2.50-3.00* |

- *Good wines for parties*
Blanc de France	FR	③	£2.00-2.50
Hungarian Country Wine			
(easy drinking)	HU	②	£2.00-2.50

- *Splashing out*
  | Champagne Louis Raymond | FR | ① | £7.50-8.00 |

RED AND ROSÉ

- *Light and fruity wines for easy drinking at any time*
Rosé de France *(easy drinking)*	FR	③	£2.00-2.50
Il Paesano Merlot del Veneto	IT		£2.00-2.50
Rouge de France	FR		£2.00-2.50
Côtes du Ventoux Rosé			
(particularly fruity)	FR	④	£2.50-3.00*
Valpolicella	IT		£2.50-3.00
Iambol Merlot/Pamid			
(easy drinking)	BU		£2.50-3.00*
VdP de l'Hérault *(litre)*	FR		£3.00-3.50*

- *Medium-bodied wines to serve on their own or with food*

Minervois	FR	£2.50-3.00
Côtes du Ventoux *(distinctive)*	FR	£2.50-3.00
Merlot Domaine Resclause		
VdP d'Oc	FR	£2.50-3.00*
Arietta Montepulciano d'Abbruzzo	IT	£2.50-3.00*
Promesa Tinto	SP	£2.50-3.00
Clearsprings Cape Red	SA	£2.50-3.00
San Pedro	CH	£2.50-3.00*
Château Fontcaude St Chinian		
(particularly fruity)	FR	£3.00-3.50*

Cabernet Sauvignon and Cabernet blends

Lovico Suhindol Cabernet/Merlot	BU	£2.00-2.50
Claret Cuvée VE	FR	£2.50-3.00
Cabernet Sauvignon VdP d'Oc		
(particularly fruity)	FR	£2.50-3.00*
Burgas Bulgarian Cabernet		
Sauvignon	BU	£2.50-3.00*

- *Heavier wines to serve with food*

Pelican Bay Australian Red	OZ	£2.50-3.00
Steep Ridge VdP d'Oc Grenache/		
Shiraz *(distinctive)*	FR	£2.50-3.00*

Cabernet Sauvignon and Cabernet blends

Cabernet Sauvignon Reserve		
Oriachovitza *(distinctive)*	BU	£3.00-3.50*
Maxfield Vineyards Premium Red	USA	£3.00-3.50
Angove's Butterfly Ridge Cabernet/		
Shiraz	OZ	£3.50-4.00*

- *Good wines for parties*

Leziria Red Vinho Mesa Tinto		
(easy drinking)	P	£2.00-2.50
Hungarian Merlot *(easy drinking)*	HU	£2.50-3.00

WHITE

- *Fresh and light wines for easy drinking at any time*

VdP Vaucluse Blanc	FR	②	£2.00-2.50
VdP de Pyrenees Orientales *(easy drinking)*	FR	①	£2.50-3.00*
Domaine de Lalanne VdP des Côtes de Gascogne	FR	②	£2.50-3.00
Soave	IT	②	£2.50-3.00
Le Bordeaux Blanc	FR	②	£3.00-3.50

Sauvignon Blanc and Sauvignon-based wines

Andes Peak Sauvignon Blanc *(particularly fruity)*	CH	①	£3.00-3.50*
Windsor Ridge Sauvignon Blanc	OZ	①	£3.50-4.00

- *Fuller-flavoured and fruity, but still relatively dry, wines*

Misty Moorings Angoves White	OZ	②	£3.00-3.50
Windsor Ridge Semillon	OZ	②	£3.00-3.50
Hardy's RR *(particularly fruity)*	OZ	②	£3.50-4.00*

Chardonnay and Chardonnay blends

Windsor Ridge Chardonnay	OZ	③	£3.50-4.00
Hardy's Stamp Series Semillon/ Chardonnay	OZ	②	£3.50-4.00
Le Piat Chardonnay	FR	②	£4.00-4.50

- *Medium dry, very fruity, wines to serve at any time*

Romanian Cellars Riesling/Muscat	R	⑤	£2.50-3.00
Morio Muscat Rheinpfalz	GER	④	£3.00-3.50
Oppenheimer Krötenbrunnen	GER	⑤	£3.00-3.50
Jacob's Creek Medium White Riesling	OZ	④	£4.00-4.50

- **Sparkling wines for aperitifs and parties**
Asti Martini	IT	⑧	£6.00-6.50
Marquès de Monistrol Brut	SP	②	£6.00-6.50

- **Dessert or pudding wines**
St Johanner Abtey Auslese Rheinhessen	GER	⑦	£4.50-5.00

- **Good wines for parties**
Romanian Pinot Gris	RO	②	£3.00-3.50
Silver Peak Californian White *(distinctive)*	USA	②	£3.00-3.50

- **Splashing out**
Orlando Chardonnay *(particularly fruity)*	OZ	②	£5.00-5.50*

RED

- **Light and fruity wines for easy drinking at any time**
Merlot Villany	HU	£2.50-3.00
Romanian Pinot Noir	R	£3.00-3.50*
Littlewoods Côtes du Roussillon Villages	FR	£3.00-3.50
Le Piat Merlot	FR	£4.00-4.50

- **Medium-bodied wines to serve on their own or with food**
Littlewoods Claret	FR	£3.00-3.50
Littlewoods Corbières *(particularly fruity)*	FR	£3.00-3.50
Littlewoods Fitou	FR	£3.50-4.00
Jacob's Creek Red	OZ	£4.00-4.50

  Cabernet Sauvignon and Cabernet blends
Hungarian Cabernet Sauvignon	H	£2.50-3.00

Andes Peak Cabernet/Merlot	CH	£3.00-3.50
Hardy's Chiraz/Cabernet Sauvignon *(easy drinking)*	OZ	£3.50-4.00
Le Piat Cabernet Sauvignon *(particularly fruity)*	FR	£4.00-4.50

- ### *Heavier wines to serve with food*

Windsor Ridge Shiraz	OZ	£3.00-3.50*
Bairrada	P	£3.50-4.00
Rioja	SP	£4.00-4.50

Cabernet Sauvignon and Cabernet blends

| Windsor Ridge Cabernet Sauvignon | OZ | £3.50-4.00 |

- ### *Good wines for parties*

| Angoves Australian Red *(particularly fruity)* | OZ | £3.00-3.50* |
| Valpolicella | IT | £3.00-3.50 |

- ### *Splashing out*

| Marquès de Caceres Rioja *(distinctive)* | SP | £5.00-5.50* |
| A. Garrett Shiraz *(particularly fruity)* | | £5.50-6.00 |

This company operates as a wholesaler so purchases must be a minimum of 12 bottles of wine, but you can mix your case and add odd bottles over the first 12.

WHITE

- *Fresh and light wines for easy drinking at any time*

Domaine de Robinson VdP Côtes de			
Gascogne	FR	②	£3.00-3.50
Soave Folonari *(easy drinking)*	IT	②	£3.00-3.50*
Cortenova Trebbiano del Veneto			
Pasqua	IT	①	£3.00-3.50
Domaine Le Puts Blanc VdP des Côtes			
de Gascogne *(particularly fruity)*	FR	②	£3.50-4.00*
Pinot Grigio Fratelli Pasqua	IT	①	£3.50-4.00
Soave Classico Tedeschi			
(particularly fruity)	IT	②	£4.00-4.50*

Sauvignon Blanc and Sauvignon blends

Sauvignon Blanc Comte d'Ormont	FR	①	£3.50-4.00
Cheverny Blanc *(distinctive)*	FR	①	£3.50-4.00
Bordeaux Blanc Raoul Johnston	FR	①	£4.00-4.50*

- *Fuller-flavoured and fruity, but still relatively dry, wines*

Santara Dry White Conca de			
Barbera *(particularly fruity)*	SP		£3.00-3.50*
Misty Mooring White Angroves	OZ	②	£3.00-3.50
Villa Fontana Candida	IT	①	£4.00-4.50
Penfolds Bin 202 Rhine Riesling			
(particularly fruity)	OZ	③	£4.00-4.50*
Cuvée Constantin Qualitatswein			
Trocken Richter	GER	①	£4.50-5.00

Chardonnay and Chardonnay blends

Gyongyos Estate Chardonnay	HU	②	£3.00-3.50
Moldova Hincesti Chardonnay			
Hugh Ryman	MO	②	£3.00-3.50*
Chardonnay VdP d'Oc Bessière	FR	②	£3.50-4.00
Mâcon Blanc Les Chazelles	FR	②	£4.00-4.50
Cranswick Estate Chardonnay	OZ	②	£4.00-4.50

- *Medium dry, very fruity, wines to serve at any time*

Muskat/Ugni Blanc Country Wine			
(easy drinking)	BU	②	£2.50-3.00

Bockenheimer Grafenstuck Scheurebe Kabinett	GER	③	£3.50-4.00

- *Sparkling wines for aperitifs and parties*

Cristalino Cava Brut Jaume Serra	SP	①	£5.00-5.60
Angas Brut	OZ	①	£6.00-6.50
Seppelt Chardonnay Blanc de Blancs	OZ	①	£7.50-8.00

- *Dessert or pudding wine*

Muscat VdP Collines de la Moure *(distinctively fruity) (half)*	FR	⑦	£3.00-3.50*

- *Good wines for parties*

Le St Cricq Blanc de Blancs *(French bottled)*	SP	①	£2.00-2.50
Sur Lie Blanc de Blancs VdP d'Oc	FR	②	£3.00-3.50

- *Splashing out*

Domaine du Tariquet VdP des Côtes de Gascogne Cuvée Bois *(oaky)*	FR	②	£5.00-5.50*
Dometaia Vernaccia di San Gimignano	IT	①	£5.00-5.50*
Coopers Creek Sauvignon Blanc	NZ	①	£5.00-5.50

RED AND ROSÉ

- *Light and fruity wines for easy drinking at any time*

VdP de Vaucluse Robertson *(particularly fruity and easy drinking)*	FR		£3.00-3.50*
Villa Rocca Rosso	IT		£3.00-3.50

Domaine de la Presidente VdP de la Principaute d'Orange	FR		£3.00-3.50
Cheverny Rouge Oisly et Thesée	FR		£3.50-4.00
Pinot Noir Touraine	FR		£3.50-4.00
Montepulciano d'Abruzzo	IT		£3.50-4.00
Domaine le Puts Rosé	FR	②	£4.00-4.50*
Valpolicella Classico Tedeschi *(particularly fruity)*	IT		£4.00-4.50*

- ***Medium-bodied wines to serve on their own or with food***

Comte de Feynes Raoul Johnston	FR	£3.00-3.50
Chinon Rouge Les Bardons *(particularly fruity)*	FR	£3.00-3.50*
Santara Red Conca de Barbera *(easy drinking)*	SP	£3.00-3.50*
Domaine Guingal Cahors	FR	£3.00-3.50*
Fitou Les Rocailles	FR	£3.50-4.00
Syrah Fortant de France VdP d'Oc	FR	£4.00-4.50
Domaine Fouletiere Coteaux de Languedoc	FR	£4.00-4.50
Jaume Serra Penedès Resrva *(distinctive)*	SP	£4.00-4.50

Cabernet Sauvignon and Cabernet blends

Cranswick Estate Shiraz/Cabernet *(easy drinking)*	OZ	£4.00-4.50

- ***Heavier wines to serve with food***

Serradayres CRF	P	£3.00-3.50
Monestere de Trignan Côteaux du Languedoc	FR	£4.00-4.50
Alentejo Tinto Velho Fonseca *(distinctive)*	P	£4.00-4.50*

Cabernet Sauvignon and Cabernet blends

Concha y Toro Cabernet/Merlot	CH	£3.50-4.00*
Angoves Cabernet Sauvignon	OZ	£4.50-5.00

- **Good wines for parties**
    Le St Cricq Vin de Table Rouge
        (French bottled)   SP   £2.00-2.50
    Bulgarian Cabernet Sauvignon
        Russe   BU   £2.50-3.00*
    Merlot Cortenova Pasqua   IT   £2.50-3.00

- **Splashing out**
    Domaine de Sours Bordeaux
        Supérieur   FR   £5.00-5.50*
    Château de Luc Corbières   FR   £5.00-5.50*
    Lirac Château d'Aqueria   FR   £7.00-7.50*

WHITE

- **Fresh and light wines for easy drinking at any time**
    Cortese de Piemonte Vino de Tavola IT ① £3.00-3.50
    VdP du Gers   FR ② £3.00-3.50
    Santara Dry White   SP ② £3.00-3.50
    Pinot Grigio delle Tre Venezie Vino
        de Tavola   IT ② £3.50-4.00
    Domaine l'Argentier Terret VdP FR ② £3.50-4.00
    Muscadet Sèvre-et-Maine Domaine
        des Balluettes   FR ① £4.00-4.50
    Frascati Superiore Girelli
        (particularly fruity)   IT ② £4.00-4.50
    Sauvignon Blanc and Sauvignon blends
    Hungarian Sauvignon Blanc
        (particularly fruity)   HU ① £3.00-3.50

Cape Country Sauvignon	SA	①	£3.00-3.50
Bordeaux Sauvignon *(particularly fruity)*	FR	①	£3.50-4.00*
Sauvignon Blanc	CH	①	£4.00-4.50

- ***Fuller-flavoured and fruity, but still relatively dry, wines***

Cape Country Colombard KWV *(particularly fruity)*	SA	②	£3.00-3.50*
Australian Medium Dry *(oaky)*	OZ	③	£3.50-4.00
Vouvray Domaine Pouvraie	FR	②	£4.50-5.00

Chardonnay and Chardonnay blends

Chardonnay Vino de Tavola del Piemonte Fratelli Martini *(particularly fruity)*	IT	②	£3.00-3.50*
VdP du Jardin de la France Chardonnay Celliers des Samsons	FR	②	£4.00-4.50
Chardonnay del Piemonte Giordano	IT	②	£4.00-4.50*
Stellenbosch Chardonnay	SA	②	£4.00-4.50
Semillon/Chardonnay SE Australia	OZ	②	£4.00-4.50

- ***Medium dry, very fruity, wines to serve at any time***

Piesporter Michelsberg	GER	④	£3.00-3.50
Bereich Nierstein	GER	④	£3.50-4.00

- ***Sparkling wines for aperitifs and parties***

Asti Bosca	IT	⑦	£5.00-5.50
Australian Sparkling Brut	OZ	②	£5.00-5.50
Cava	SP	①	£5.50-6.00*
Sparkling Chardonnay	FR	②	£6.00-6.50
Crémant de Bougogne Cave de Lugny	FR	②	£7.00-7.50*
Blenheim Sparkling Wine	NZ	②	£7.00-7.50*

- ***Goods wines for parties***

Marks & Spencer House White, La Mancha *(French bottled)*	SP	②	£3.00-3.50

VdP des Côtes de Gascogne			
Plaimont *(particularly fruity)*	FR	②	£3.00-3.50*
Soave Girelli *(litre)*	IT	①	£4.00-4.50

- **Splashing out**

Jeune Vigne	FR	②	£5.00-5.50
Rothbury Estate Chardonnay/			
Semillon *(particularly fruity)*	OZ	②	£5.00-5.50*
Petit Chablis La Chablisiènne	FR	②	£5.50-6.00*
Sancerre La Charmette *(particularly*			
fruity)	FR	①	£6.00-6.50*
Chablis La Chablisiènne	FR	②	£7.00-7.50*

RED AND ROSÉ

- *Light and fruity wines for easy drinking at any time*

Domaine de St Pierre VdP de		
l'Hérault	FR	£3.00-3.50
Barbera Piemonte Fratelli Martini	IT	£3.00-3.50
Gamay VdP des Coteaux de		
l'Ardèche	FR	£3.50-4.00
Valpolicella Classico	IT	£3.50-4.00
Beaujolais	FR	£4.00-4.50*
Italian Table Red *(easy drinking)*	IT	£4.00-4.50
Australian Rosé *(particularly fruity)*	OZ ②	£4.00-4.50*

- *Medium-bodied wines to serve on their own or with food*

Montepulciano d'Abrusso	IT	£3.00-3.50*
Fitou *(particularly fruity)*	FR	£3.50-4.00*

Cabernet Sauvignon and Cabernet blends

Cabernet Sauvignon VdP d'Oc		
(particularly fruity)	FR	£3.00-3.50
Hungarian Cabernet Sauvignon	HU	£3.00-3.50

Cabernet Sauvignon Svischtov		
Region *(particularly fruity)*	BU	£3.00-3.50*
Château Lacousse Classic Claret	FR	£4.00-4.50
Domaine Montrose	FR	£4.00-4.50*

• *Heavier wines to serve with food*

Rioja	SP	£3.50-4.00
Domaine Roche Blanche		
(particularly fruity)	FR	£4.00-4.50*
Dão Garrafeira Cave Alianca		
(particularly fruity)	PO	£4.00-4.50*
Shiraz/Cabernet McWilliams		
(particularly fruity)	OZ	£4.00-4.50

• *Good wines for parties*

Domaine St Pierre VdP de		
l'Hérault *(easy drinking)*	FR	£3.00-3.50
Australian Red Pheasant Gully		
Shiraz *(particularly fruity and*		
easy drinking)	OZ	£4.00-4.50

• *Splashing out*

Selection Speciale Bordeaux		
Baron Philippe de Rothschild	FR	£5.00-5.50
Costers del Segre Raimat	SP	£5.00-5.50
Coonawarra Cabernet Sauvignon	OZ	£5.00-5.50*
Vino Nobile di Montepulciano		
Girelli	IT	£6.00-6.50*
Len Evans Cabernet Sauvignon	OZ	£6.00-6.50*

Morrisons

WHITE

- *Fresh and light wines for easy drinking at any time*

VdP de Jardin de la France	FR	②	£2.50-3.00
Trebbiano del Vigneti Del Sole	IT	②	£2.50-3.00
Romanian Cellarmasters White	RO	②	£2.50-3.00
VdP des Côtes de Gascogne			
(*particularly fruity*)	FR	②	£3.00-3.50
VdP Terret (*distinctive*)	FR	②	£3.00-3.50*
Est! Est!! Est!!!	IT	②	£3.00-3.50
Frascati Superiore Orsole	IT	②	£3.00-3.50
Servus Burgenland (*easy drinking*)	A	③	£3.00-3.50
Château St Gallier Graves	FR	②	£4.00-4.50*

Sauvignon Blanc and Sauvignon-based wines

Romanian Sauvignon Blanc	RO	①	£2.50-3.00
Sauvignon de Touraine	FR	①	£3.00-3.50
Sauvignon VdP d'Oc Lurton	FR	①	£3.00-3.50
Sauvignon Blanc Dulong Bordeaux	FR	①	£3.50-4.00
Santa Carolina Sauvignon Blanc	CH	②	£4.00-4.50

- *Fuller-flavoured and fruity, but still relatively dry, wines*

Bulgarian Country White	BU	④	£2.50-3.00
Fair Cape Chenin Blanc	SA	③	£2.50-3.00
VdP des Pyranees Orientale Capage			
Muscat (*distinctively fruity*)	FR	②	£3.00-3.50*
Woomera Vale Australian White	OZ	②	£3.00-3.50*

Chardonnay and Chardonnay blends

Bulgarian Chardonnay	BU	②	£2.50-3.00
Chardonnay Teresa Rizzi			
(*easy-drinking*)	IT	②	£3.00-3.50
Chais Cuxac Chardonnay	FR	②	£3.50-4.00*

Glenn Ellen Chardonnay
  (particulalry fruity)   USA   ②   £4.00-4.50
Penfolds Bin 21 Semillon/
  Chardonnay *(particularly fruity)*   OZ   ②   £4.00-4.50*
Barramundi Semillon/
  Chardonnay   OZ   ②   £4.00-4.50
Lindemans Chardonnay   OZ   ②   £4.50-5.00

- **Medium dry, very fruity, wines to serve at any time**
  Flonheimer Adelberg Kabinett
    (easy drinking)   GER   ④   £2.50-3.00
  Wiltinger Scharzberg Spätlese
    (particularly fruity)   GER   ④   £3.00-3.50*
  Leiwener Klostergarten Auslese   GER   ⑥   £4.00-4.50*

- **Sparkling wines for aperitifs and parties**
  Asti Gianni   IT   ⑦   £4.50-5.00
  Seppelt Great Western Brut   OZ   ②   £4.50-5.00
  Cristalino Brut *(particuarly fruity)*   SP   ①   £5.00-5.50*
  Seaview Brut   OZ   ②   £5.50-6.00
  Asti Martini   IT   ⑦   £6.00-6.50
  Freixenet Brut Rosé   SP   ②   £6.00-6.50
  Gratien & Meyer Brut   FR   ②   £6.00-6.50

- **Dessert or pudding wine**
  Moscatel de Valencia   SP   ⑧   £3.00-3.50

- **Good wines for parties**
  Gabbia D'Oro Vino Bianco   IT   ③   £2.00-2.50
  Comtesse de Lorancy *(easy drinking)*
    (French bottled)   EU   ②   £2.50-3.00
  Côtes de Roussillon Blanc *(easy
    drinking)*   FR   ②   £2.50-3.00

- **Splashing out**
  Nicole d'Aurigny Champagne   FR   ①   £9.00-9.50*

RED

- *Light and fruity wines for easy drinking at any time*

Côtes de Ventoux	FR	£2.50-3.00
Le Cellier La Chonf Minervois	FR	£2.50-3.00
Merlot Vigneti del Sole	IT	£2.50-3.00
Montepulciano d'Abruzzo	IT	£2.50-3.00*
Romanian Pinot Noir	R	£2.50-3.00*
Fair Cape Cinsault	SA	£2.50-3.00
Coteaux du Languedoc (*particularly fruity*)	FR	£3.00-3.50*
Beaujolais Champelos	FR	£3.00-3.50

- *Medium-bodied wines to serve on their own or with food*

Les Fenouillets Corbières	FR	£2.50-3.00
Romanian Cellarmasters Red (*easy drinking and distinctive*)	RO	£2.50-3.00
Côtes de Rousillon Villages	FR	£2.50-3.00
Morrisons Rioja	SP	£2.50-3.00*
Faugères	FR	£3.00-3.50
Côtes-du-Rhône Village Epitalon (*particularly fruity*)	FR	£3.00-3.50*
Valdezaro Chilean Red	CH	£3.00-3.50
Blossom Hill Red	USA	£3.00-3.50
Côtes du Buzet (*particularly fruity*)	FR	£3.50-4.00*
Romanian Reserve Merlot	RO	£3.50-4.00
Glen Ellen Merlot (*particularly fruity*)	USA	£4.00-4.50*

Cabernet Sauvignon and Cabernet blends

Bulgarian Cabernet Sauvignon	BU	£2.50-3.00
Cabernet Sauvignon VdP d'Oc	FR	£3.00-3.50*
Morrisons Claret	FR	£3.00-3.50
Chais Cuxac VdP d'Oc Cabernet Sauvignon (*particularly fruity*)	FR	£3.50-4.00*

| Rocca Delle Macie Classico | IT | £4.50-5.00 |

- **_Heavier wines to serve with food_**

Soveral Portuguese Red	P	£2.00-2.50
Moroccan Red _(distinctively fruity)_	M	£2.50-3.00
Jaume Serra Tempranillo _(easy drinking and fruity)_	SP	£3.00-3.50*
Borges Bairrada Reserva	P	£3.00-3.50
Woomera Vale Australian Red	OZ	£3.00-3.50
Torres Sangredetoro _(distinctive)_	SP	£3.50-4.00
Campo Viejo Rioja	SP	£4.00-4.50

Cabernet and Cabernet blends

Romanian Cabernet _(distinctive)_	RO	£3.00-3.50
Santa Carolina Cabernet Sauvignon _(particularly fruity)_	CH	£3.50-4.00*
Hanwood Estate Cabernet Sauvignon _(particularly fruity)_	OZ	£4.00-4.50
Penfolds Bin 2	OZ	£4.00-4.50*

- **_Good wines for parties_**

VdP Pyrenees Orientales	FR	£2.00-2.50
VdP d'Oc Merlot _(particularly fruity)_	FR	£2.50-3.00
VdP de Jardin de la France	FR	£2.50-3.00

- **_Splashing out_**

| Campo Viejo Rioja Reserva | SP | £5.00-5.50* |
| Margaux | FR | £8.00-8.50* |

Normans

WHITE

- **_Fresh and light wines for easy drinking at any time_**

| Cave De Masse | FR ③ | £2.50-3.00 |

| Gallo Sauvignon Blanc | USA | ② | £4.00-4.50 |

- *Fuller-flavoured and fruity, but still relatively dry, wines*
  Chardonnay and Chardonnay-based wines

Hungarian Chardonnay	HU	②	£2.50-3.00
Chardonnay del Veneto	IT	②	£3.00-3.50
Le Piat Chardonnay	FR	②	£4.00-4.50
Montana Chardonnay	NZ	②	£4.50-5.00*

- *Medium dry, very fruity, wine to serve at any time*

| Gallo Chenin Blanc | USA | ④ | £3.50-4.00 |

- *Sparkling wine for aperitifs and parties*

| Asti Martini | IT | ⑦ | £6.00-6.50 |

RED

- *Light and fruity wines for easy drinking at any time*

Hungarian Merlot	HU	£2.50-3.00
Romanian Pinot Noir	RO	£2.50-3.00
Le Piat Merlot	FR	£4.00-4.50

- *Medium-bodied wines to serve on their own or with food*

Bulgarian Cabernet Sauvignon	BU	£3.00-3.50
Fitou	FR	£3.50-4.00
Cape Country Cabernet Sauvignon	SA	£3.50-4.00
Le Piat Cabernet Sauvignon		
(particularly fruity)	FR	£4.00-4.50
Harveys No.1 Claret	FR	£4.50-5.00

- *Heavier wines to serve with food*

Henry Lindeman Shiraz Cabernet	OZ	£3.50-4.00
St Emilion	FR	£4.50-5.00
Montana Cabernet Sauvignon	NZ	£4.50-5.00

Oddbins

WHITE

- *Fresh and light wines for easy drinking at any time*

VdP des Côtes de Thau Terret *(easy drinking)*	FR	①	£3.00-3.50
Pinot Grigio Vin de Tavola Casona	IT	②	£3.00-3.50*
Castillo di Olite Navarra	SP	②	£3.00-3.50
VdP d'Oc Domaine de Bachellery	FR	②	£3.50-4.00
Bodegas Montecillo Viña Cumbrero Blanco	SP	②	£3.50-4.00
Muscadet Domaine de la Grange	FR	①	£4.00-4.50*
Trois Mouline VdP d'Oc	FR	②	£4.00-4.50

Sauvignon Blanc and Sauvignon blends

Caliterra Sauvignon Blanc *(particularly fruity)*	CH	①	£3.50-4.00
Lurton VdP d'Oc Sauvignon	FR	①	£3.50-4.00
Sauvignon Rueda *(particularly fruity)*	SP	①	£4.00-4.50*

- *Fuller-flavoured and fruity, but still relatively dry, wines*

Glenroth Dry White	OZ	②	£3.00-3.50
Eden Valley Riesling	OZ	④	£3.00-3.50
Glen Ellen Proprietors White Sonoma	USA	②	£3.00-3.50
Barossa Valley Estates Dry White	OZ	②	£3.50-4.00
The Monterey Vineyard Dry White	USA	②	£3.50-4.00
Torrontes & Treixadura Solana *(distinctive)*	SP	②	£4.00-4.50

Chardonnay and Chardonnay blends

Chardonnay VdP des Côtes Catalanes	FR	②	£3.00-3.50*

Chardonnay Hugh Ryman
 Moldova *(particularly fruity)*   MO ② £3.00-3.50*
Chapel Hill Chardonnay   HU ② £3.00-3.50
Lindemans Colombard/
 Chardonnay S.E.Australia   OZ ② £3.50-4.00
Killawarra Chardonnay   OZ ② £3.50-4.00*
Barossa Valley Estates Chardonnay   OZ ② £3.50-4.00
Hardy's Semillon/Chardonnay   OZ ② £3.50-4.00
Caliterra Chardonnay *(oaky)*   CH ② £4.00-4.50*
Glen Ellen Proprietors Reserve
 Chardonnay *(particularly fruity)* USA ② £4.00-4.50*
Hardy's Nottage Hill Chardonnay   OZ ② £4.00-4.50*

- *Medium dry, very fruity, wines to serve at any time*
 Bulgarian Country Wine Muscat/
  Ugni Blanc *(easy drinking)*   BU ③ £2.50-3.00
 St Ursula Pinot Blanc   GER ③ £4.00-4.50

- *Sparkling wines for aperitifs and parties*
 Seaview Brut   OZ ② £5.50-6.00
 Angas Brut Rosé   OZ ② £6.00-6.50
 Segura Viudas Reserva   SP ① £6.00-6.50
 Seppelts Premier Cuvée   OZ ② £6.50-7.00
 Conde de Caralt Blancs de Blanc   SP ① £6.50-7.00
 Montana Lindauer Brut   NZ ② £7.00-7.50
 Seaview Pinot/Chardonnay
  McLaren Vale   OZ ② £7.50-8.00*

- *Dessert or pudding wine*
 Tolleys Late Harvest Muscat   OZ ⑧ £3.50-4.00

- *Good wines for parties*
 VdP des Côtes de Gascogne   FR ② £3.00-3.50
 Chardonnay Vino da Tavola Casona
  (easy drinking)   IT ② £3.00-3.50

- *Splashing out*
  Caliterra Casablanc Chardonnay   CH   ②   £5.00-5.50

RED AND ROSÉ

- *Light and fruity wines for easy drinking at any time*

Riva Sangiovese di Romagna	IT	£2.50-3.00
Vega de Moriz Cencabel Tinto *(particularly fruity)*	SP	£2.50-3.00
Château de Jau VdP des Côtes Catalanes *(particularly fruity)*	FR	£3.00-3.50*
Le Radical VdP de Vaucluse	FR	£3.50-4.00
Santa Rita Cabernet Sauvignon Rosé	CH ②	£4.00-4.50
Valpolicella Classico Masi	IT	£4.50-5.00*

- *Medium-bodied wines to serve on their own or with food*

VdP des Coteaux du Quercy	FR	£3.00-3.50
Faugères Jeanjean	FR	£3.00-3.50
Domaine de la Grange VdP du Vallée de Paradis	FR	£3.00-3.50
Côtes-du-Rhônes Enclave des Papes	FR	£3.00-3.50
Merlot Lovico Suhindol Region *(particularly fruity)*	BU	£3.00-3.50
Volcanic Hills Merlot Vaskeresztes Region *(particularly fruity)*	HU	£3.00-3.50
VdP des Coteaux de Cabrerisse	FR	£3.50-4.00
Casa de la Viña Valdepeñas Cencibel *(particularly fruity)*	SP	£4.00-4.50*
Bodegas Montecillo Viña Cumbrero Tinto *(particularly fruity)*	SP	£4.50-5.00*

Carbernet Sauvignon and Cabernet blends

Vintage Blend Reserve Cabernet Sauvignon/Merlot Lovico Suhindol Region *(oaky)*	BU	£3.00-3.50
Santa Rita 120 Cabernet Sauvignon *(particularly fruity)*	CH	£4.00-4.50*

- *Heavier wines to serve with food*

Vincola Navarra Las Campanas Crianza	SP	£3.50-4.00
Peter Lehmann Vine Vale Shiraz	OZ	£4.00-4.50

Cabernet Sauvignon and Cabernet blends

Glenroth Shiraz Cabernet	OZ	£3.00-3.50
Coldridge Estate Shiraz/Cabernet	OZ	£3.50-4.00
Killawarra Cabernet Sauvignon	OZ	£3.50-4.00

- *Good wines for parties*

Cuvée du Patron Borie-Manoux	FR	£2.50-3.00
Taraclia de Moldova Cabernet Sauvignon	MO	£3.00-3.50*
Valley Estates Dry Red	OZ	£3.00-3.50

- *Splashing out*

Mount Hurtle Shiraz	OZ	£6.00-6.50
Côtes-du-Rhône Guigal	FR	£6.00-6.50

WHITE

- *Fresh and light wines for easy drinking at any time*

Safeway Sicilian Dry White	IT	②	£2.50-3.00*

Safeway Vino de Valencia	SP	②	£2.50-3.00
Safeway Côtes du Luberon Ryman *(particularly fruity)*	FR	②	£3.00-3.50
La Coume de Peyre VdP des Côtes de Gascogne	FR	②	£3.00-3.50*
Riva Trebbiano di Romagna	IT	①	£3.00-3.50
Safeway Orvieto Classico Secco *(particularly fruity)*	IT	②	£3.50-4.00
I Frari Bianca di Custoza Santi	IT	②	£3.50-4.00*
Grave del Fruili Pinot Grigio	IT	②	£4.00-4.50*

Sauvignon Blanc and Sauvignon blends

Sauvignon VdP du Jardin de la France	FR	①	£2.50-3.00
Sauvignon Blanc Vredendal	SA	①	£3.00-3.50
Safeway Bergerac Sauvignon *(particularly fruity)*	FR	①	£3.50-4.00*
Château de Plantier Entre-deux-Mers *(particularly fruity)*	FR	①	£3.50-4.00*
Lurton Sauvignon VdP d'Oc	FR	①	£4.00-4.50*
Domaine de Mallardeau Côtes de Duras *(particularly fruity)*	FR	②	£4.00-4.50*

- *Fuller-flavoured and fruity, but still relatively dry, wines*

Safeway Country Wine Russe	BU	④	£2.50-3.00
Safeway Dry Muscat Nagyrede *(distinctively fruity)*	HU	②	£2.50-3.00
Safeway Australian Dry White	OZ	②	£2.50-3.00
Swartland Steen	SA	②	£3.00-3.50
Safeway Semillon Riverina	OZ	②	£3.00-3.50
St Ursula Ryman Riesling Trocken *(particularly fruity)*	GER	②	£3.50-4.00*
Lenz Moser Pinot Blanc Kabinett Trocken	A	②	£3.50-4.00
Czech Pinot Blanc	CZ	②	£3.50-4.00
Grave del Fruili Pinot Grigio	IT	①	£4.00-4.50*

Chardonnay and Chardonnay blends:

Gyongyos Estate Chardonnay	HU	②	£3.00-3.50
Hincesti Chardonnay Ryman *(oaky)*	MO	②	£3.00-3.50*
La Monferrine Chardonnay del Piemonte	IT	②	£3.50-4.00*
Safeway Semillon/Chardonnay	OZ	②	£3.50-4.00*
Hardy's Nottage Hill	OZ	②	£4.00-4.50*
Danie de Wet Chardonnay Sur Lie	SA	②	£4.50-5.00*

- *Medium dry, very fruity wines to serve at any time*

Moscato d'Asti *(semi-sparkling)*	IT	⑤	£2.50-3.00
Safeway Kabinett Rheinpfalz	GER	④	£3.00-3.50
Ruppertsberger Nussbien Riesling Kabinett Rheinpfalz	GER	④	£3.50-4.00

- *Sparkling wines for aperitifs and parties*

Safeway Asti	IT	⑦	£4.50-5.00
Safeway Cava	SP	①	£5.00-5.50
Asti Martini	IT	⑦	£6.00-6.50
Safeway Saumur	FR	①	£6.00-6.50
Le Grand Pavillon de Boschendal Cuvée Brut	SA	①	£6.00-6.50*
Seppelt Premier Cuvée Brut	OZ	②	£6.00-6.50
Blanquette de Limoux *(organic)*	FR	④	£7.00-7.50*
Lindauer Brut	NZ	②	£7.00-7.50

Chardonnay

Safeway Crémant de Bourgogne Brut	FR	②	£6.50-7.00

- *Dessert or pudding wine*

Muscat Cuvée Jose Sala	FR	⑤	£3.50-4.00*

- *Good wines for parties*

Safeway La Mancha	SP	②	£2.50-3.00
Safeway Hungarian Country Wine	H	②	£2.50-3.00

Hincesti Feteasca Moldova Ryman			
(particularly easy drinking)	MO	②	£3.00-3.50*

- ### Splashing out
Domaine de Rivoyre Chardonnay			
VdP d'Oc	FR	②	£5.00-5.50*
Wakefield White Clare	OZ	②	£5.00-5.50*
Hunter Valley Chardonnay *(oaky)*	OZ	②	£5.00-5.50*
The Millton Vineyard Chardonnay/			
Semillon Gisborne *(organic)*	NZ	②	£5.00-5.50*
St Ursula Oak Aged Pinot Blanc			
Rheinhessen	GER	②	£5.50-6.00*

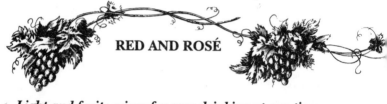

RED AND ROSÉ

- ### Light and fruity wines for easy drinking at any time
Cheateau des Blanes Côtes du		
Roussillon	FR	£2.50-3.00
Country Wine Pinot and Merlot		
Sliven Region	BU	£2.50-3.00
Safeways Merlot Villany	HU	£2.50-3.00
Czech Frankovka *(very easy drinking)*	CZ	£2.50-3.00
Safeway Côtes du Roussillon		
Villages	FR	£3.00-3.50
Merlot VdP des Coteaux de		
l'Ardèche	FR	£3.00-3.50*
Safeway Chianti	IT	£3.00-3.50
Young Vatted Tempranillo La		
Mancha *(particularly fruity)*	SP	£3.00-3.50
Safeway Romanian Merlot	RO	£3.00-3.50

Cabernet Sauvignon
Hungarian Country Red Kiskoros	HU	£2.50-3.00
Safeway Bergerac	FR	£3.00-3.50*

Cabernet Sauvignon Villany	HU		£3.00-3.50
Cabernet Sauvignon Rosé			
Nagyrede	HU	②	£3.00-3.50*
Château Canet Entre-deux-Mers			
Rosé *(organic)*	FR	①	£4.00-4.50*

• *Medium-bodied wines to serve on their own or with food*

Safeway VdP l'Ardèche	FR	£2.50-3.00
Safeway Sicilian Red	IT	£2.50-3.00*
Don Darias *(oaky)*	SP	£2.50-3.00
Young Vatted Merlot	BU	£2.50-3.00*
Great Plains Kekfrankos	HU	£3.00-3.50
Safeway Côtes-du-Rhône	FR	£3.00-3.50
Safeway Côtes du Luberon	FR	£3.00-3.50
Safeway Côtes du Roussillon		
Villages *(easy drinking)*	FR	£3.00-3.50
Mavrud Assenovgrad *(distinctive)*	BU	£3.00-3.50
Merlot Reserve Stambulovo	BU	£3.00-3.50
Château la Foret Bordeaux	FR	£3.50-4.00
Abbaye de Tholomies Minervois	FR	£3.50-4.00
Château de Belesta Côtes du		
Roussillon *(particularly fruity)*	FR	£3.50-4.00*
Casa del Campo Syrah Mendoza	AR	£3.50-4.00
Château Joanny Côtes-du-Rhône	FR	£4.00-4.50*
Safeways Château de Caraguilhes		
Corbières *(organic)*	FR	£4.00-4.50

Cabernet Sauvignon and Cabernet blends

Young Vatted Cabernet Sauvignon	BU	£2.50-3.00
Krazen Vineyard Cabernet		
Sauvignon Russe *(particularly*		
fruity)	BU	£3.00-3.50*
Côtes de Duras *(oaky)*	FR	£3.50-4.00
Agramont Tempranillo/Cabernet		
Navarra *(particularly fruity)*	SP	£4.00-4.50*
Médoc Oak-aged Bordeaux	FR	£4.00-4.50

- *Heavier wines to serve with food*
  - Safeway Oak Aged Valdepeñas
    Riserva   SP   £3.00-3.50*
  - Casa de la Viña Cencibel
    Valdepeñas   SP   £3.00-3.50
  - Safeway Bairrada   P   £3.50-4.00*
  - Jacob's Creek Dry Red   OZ   £4.00-4.50

  Cabernet Sauvignon and Cabernet blends
  - Australian Cabernet Sauvignon   OZ   £3.50-4.00
  - Penfolds Bin 2 Shiraz/Mourvedre   OZ   £4.00-4.50*

- *Good wines for parties*
  - Penfolds Bin 2 Shiraz/Mataro SE
    Australia *(rich and fruity)*   OZ   £2.00-2.50*
  - Safeway Corbières   FR   £2.50-3.00*
  - Safeway Hungarian Country Wine
    *(particularly fruity and easy
    drinking)*   HU   £2.50-3.00*

- *Splashing out*
  - Penfolds Koonunga Hill Shiraz/
    Cabernet Sauvignon   OZ   £5.00-5.50*
  - Moondah Brook Cabernet
    Sauvignon   OZ   £6.00-6.50*
  - Domaine Barret Crozes Hermitage
    (particularly fruity)   FR   £6.50-7.00*

Sainsbury

WHITE

- *Fresh and light wines for easy drinking at any time*
  - Vino de la Tierra Blanco   SP ②   £2.50-3.00

Sainsbury's Sicilian White	IT	②	£2.50-3.00
Sainsbury's Baden Dry	GER	①	£2.50-3.00
Sainsbury's VdP des Côtes de Gascogne Domaines Bordes	FR	①	£3.00-3.50
Do Campo Branco *(distinctive)*	P	②	£3.00-3.50*
Sainsbury's South African Chenin Blanc	SA	②	£3.00-3.50
Château l'Ortolan Entre-deux-Mers *(particularly fruity)*	FR	①	£3.50-4.00*
Sainsbury's Côtes-du-Rhône	FR	②	£3.50-4.00
Sainsbury's Orvieto Classico Secco Merrill *(particularly fruity)*	IT	②	£3.50-4.00*
Chello Vinho Verde Seco Sogrape *(particularly fruity)*	P	①	£3.50-4.00
Frascati Superiore Cantine San Marco	IT	①	£4.50-5.00*

Sauvignon Blanc and Sauvignon-based wines

Sainsbury's Touraine Sauvignon Blanc *(particularly fruity)*	FR	①	£3.00-3.50*
Sauvignon Blanc Rueda Hermanos Lurton	SP	①	£4.00-4.50*

- *Fuller-flavoured and fruity, but still relatively dry, wines*

Chapel Hill Irsai Oliver Balatonboglar *(distintive)*	HU	②	£2.50-3.00
Sainsbury's Rioja Blanco	SP	②	£3.00-3.50
Santa Sara *(particularly fruity)*	P	①	£3.50-4.00*
Sainsbury's Frascati *(particularly fruity)*	IT	②	£3.50-4.00
Sainsbury's Australian Semillon	OZ	②	£3.50-4.00*

Chardonnay and Chardonnay blends

Chardonnay Hincesti Moldova	MO	②	£3.00-3.50
Gyongyos Estate Chardonnay	H	②	£3.50-4.00
Sainsbury's Chardonnay delle Tre Venezie	IT	②	£3.50-4.00

Vegelegen Chardonnay Coastal Region *(oaky)*	SA	②	£3.50-4.00*
Caliterra Semillon Chardonnay	CH	②	£3.50-4.00
Sainsbury's SE Australia Chenin/Chardonnay	OZ	②	£3.50-4.00
Sainsbury's Australian Chardonnay	OZ	②	£3.50-4.00
Chardonnay VdP d'Oc Ryman	FR	②	£4.00-4.50*
Chais Baumières Chardonnay VdP d'Oc	FR	②	£4.00-4.50*

- *Medium dry, very fruity, wines to serve at any time*

St Georg Morio-Muscat Pfalz	GER	④	£2.50-3.00*
Sainsbury's Vinho Verde	P	④	£3.00-3.50
Sainsbury's Kabinett Rheinhessen Dalsheimer Burg Rodenstein	GER	③	£3.00-3.50
Sainsbury's Oppenheimer Krötenbrunnen Kabinett Rheinhessen	GER	⑤	£3.00-3.50
Sainsbury's Wiltinger Scharzberg Kabinett	GER	③	£3.00-3.50
Lily Farm Vineyard Muscat Barossa Valley *(distinctively fruity)*	OZ	④	£3.50-4.00*

- *Sparkling wines for aperitifs and parties*

Sainsbury's Cava	SP	②	£5.00-5.50
Sainsbury's Australian Sparkling Wine	OZ	②	£5.00-5.50
Sainsbury's Sparkling Saumur	FR	①	£5.50-6.00*
Sainsbury's Sparkling Chardonnay	FR	②	£5.50-6.00*
Asti Martini	IT	⑦	£5.50-6.00
Angas Brut	OZ	①	£6.00-6.50

- *Dessert or pudding wine*

Sainsbury's Muscat de St Jean de Minervois *(half)*	FR	⑧	£3.00-3.50

- **Good wines for parties**

Sainsbury's Hungarian Country wine Balatonboglar *(easy drinking and fruity)*	HU	①	£2.50-3.00*
Sainsbury's VdP du Gers	FR	②	£3.00-3.50
Sainsbury's Pinot Grigio Atesino *(easy drinking)*	IT	②	£3.00-3.50

- **Splashing out**

Chardonnay Atesino Barrique Aged Vino da Tavola *(oaky)*	IT	②	£5.00-5.50*
Chapel Hill Chardonnay Balatonboglar *(oaky)*	HU	②	£5.00-5.50
Mitchelton Reserve Marsanne Goulburn Valley	OZ	②	£6.00-6.50*
Menetou-Salon Domaine Henry Pelle	FR	①	£6.00-6.50*

RED AND ROSÉ

- **Light and fruity wines for easy drinking at any time**

Sainsbury's Sicilian Red	IT	£2.50-3.00
Sainsbury's Touraine Gamay *(particularly fruity)*	FR	£3.00-3.50
Sainsbury's Gamay VdP des Coteaux des Baronnies	FR	£3.00-3.50*
Sainsbury's VdP de la Dordogne	FR	£3.00-3.50*
Moldova Pinot Noir	MO	£3.00-3.50
Moldova Codru Cabernet and Merlot Cricova	MO	£3.00-3.50*
Sainsbury's Romanian Pinot Noir	RO	£3.00-3.50*
Sainsbury's Teroldego Rotaliano Merrill *(particularly fruity)*	IT	£3.50-4.00*

Sainsbury's Chilean Merlot San
Fernando   CH   £4.00-4.50*

- *Medium-bodied wines to serve on their own or with food*

    Vino de la Tierra Tinto   SP   £2.50-3.00
    Sainsbury's Bulgarian Country Red BU   £2.50-3.00
    Sainsbury's Valpolicella Classico
        Negarine   IT   £3.00-3.50
    Sainsbury's Campo Tinto *(easy*
        drinking)   P   £3.00-3.50*
    Sainsbury's Bourgueil   FR   £3.50-4.00*
    Sainsbury's Copertino Riserva   IT   £3.50-4.00
    Bright Bothers Merlot *(easy drinking)* P   £3.50-4.00*
    Domaine du Reverend Corbières   FR   £4.00-4.50*

    Cabernet Sauvignon and Cabernet blends
    Sainsbury's Country Red Cabernet
        Sauvignon/Cinsault Russe   BU   £2.50-3.00
    Moldova Codru Cabernet
        Sauvignon and Merlot   MO   £3.00-3.50*
    Sainsbury's Graves Selection Louis
        Vialard   FR   £3.50-4.00*
    Château Moysson Bel Air Bordeaux
        Rouge   FR   £4.00-4.50*
    Cabernet Sauvignon Atesino
        Barrique Aged *(fruity and oaky)* IT   £4.50-5.00

- *Heavier wines to serve with food*

    Sainsbury's Arruda   P   £2.50-3.00
    Sainsbury's Alentejo   P   £3.00-3.50*
    Sainsbury's Douro *(distinctive)* P   £3.00-3.50
    Sainsbury's Rioja Crianza Bodegas Olarra
        (oaky)   SP   £3.50-4.00
    Herdade de Santa Marta Alentejo   P   £4.00-4.50*
    Sainsbury's Chilean Merlot San
        Fernando   CH   £4.00-4.50*

Cabernet Sauvignon and Cabernet blends

Bright Brothers Cabernet Sauvignon *(distinctive)*	P		£3.50-4.00
Sainsbury's Navarra Tempranillo Cabernet Sauvignon	SP		£3.50-4.00
Caliterra Cabernet/Merlot	CH		£3.50-4.00
Sainsbury's Australian ShirazCabernet	OZ		£3.50-4.00*

- *Good wines for parties*

Sainsbury's VdP d'Oc Ryman	FR		£2.50-3.00
Sainsbury's Hungarian Cabernet Sauvignon Rosé Nagyrede	HU	②	£3.00-3.50
Sainsbury's Faugères	FR		£3.00-3.50*
Sainsbury's La Mancha Castillo de Alhambra	SP		£3.00-3.50*
Sainsbury's Cahors	FR		£3.00-3.50

- *Splashing out*

Mount Hurtle Shiraz	OZ	£5.00-5.50*
Cooks Hawkes Bay Cabernet Merlot	NZ	£5.00-5.50*
Quinta da Bacalhoa	P	£6.00-6.50*
Saumur Champigny Domaine des Haut Sanziers	FR	£6.50-7.00*

Somerfield

This company also owns Gateway, Food Giant and SoLo and their wine lists are based on this.

WHITE

- *Fresh and light wines for easy drinking at any time*

VdP des Coteaux de l'Ardèche	FR	①	£2.50-3.00

Château Tour de Montredon Corbières Blanc	FR	①	£3.00-3.50
Lazio Bianco Pallavicini	IT	②	£3.00-3.50
Somerfield Bairrada Branco Caves Alianca	P	①	£3.00-3.50
Les Domaines Grassa VdP des Côtes de Gascogne *(particularly fruity)*	FR	②	£3.50-4.00*
Soave Classico Vigneti Montegrande Pasqua *(particularly fruity)*	IT	①	£3.50-4.00
Somerfield Frascati	IT	②	£3.50-4.00

Sauvignon Blanc and Sauvignon-based wines

Somerfield Sauvignon Blanc Canepa	CH	①	£3.00-3.50
Somerfield Sauvignon Blanc	OZ	①	£4.00-4.50

- *Fuller-flavoured and fruity, but still relatively dry, wines*

Somerfield Baden Dry	GER	③	£3.00-3.50
Somerfield Australian Dry White	OZ	②	£3.00-3.50*
Pinot Blanc Trocken Gallerei Reinpfalz St Ursula	GER	②	£3.50-4.00
Rioja Blanco Mariscol	SP	②	£4.00-4.50*

Chardonnay and Chardonnay blends

Hincesti Moldovan Chardonnay *(particularly fruity)*	MO	②	£3.00-3.50*
Somerfield Chardonnay del Piemonte	IT	②	£3.50-4.00
Chardonnay Domaine de la Tuilerie VdP d'Oc	FR	②	£4.00-4.50
Mâcon Blanc Villages, G. Desire	FR	②	£4.00-4.50
Penfold's Bin 21 Semillon/ Chardonnay *(paticularly fruity)*	OZ	②	£4.00-4.50*

- *Medium dry, very fruity, wines to serve at any time*

Bulgarian Riesling/Misket	BU	④	£2.50-3.00
Niersteiner Spiegelberg Kabinett	GER	④	£3.00-3.50*

- *Sparkling wines for aperitifs and parties*

Seppelt Great Western Brut Reserve	OZ	②	£5.00-5.50
Somerfield Cava	SP	②	£5.00-5.50*
Asti Martini	IT	⑦	£6.00-6.50
Crémant de Bourgogne Cave de Lugny	FR	②	£7.00-7.50*

- *Dessert or pudding wine*

Somerfield Moscatel de Valencia *(particularly fruity)*	SP	⑦	£3.00-3.50

- *Good wines for parties*

Somerfield Pinot Grigio del Veneto Pasqua	IT	②	£3.00-3.50
Chenin Blanc Simonsvlei Co-op	SA	①	£3.00-3.50*

- *Splashing out*

Somerfield Chablis	FR	①	£6.00-6.50
Wente Chardonnay	USA	②	£6.50-7.00*

RED

- *Light and fruity wines for easy drinking at any time*

Somerfield Côtes de Rousillon JeanJean	FR	£2.50-3.00
Somerfield Merlot del Veneto Pasqua	IT	£2.50-3.00
Merlot Domaine de la Magdelaine VdP des Collines de la Moure Côtes du Marmandais	FR	£3.00-3.50
Sangiovese di Romagna Fabbiano	IT	£3.00-3.50*
Valpolicella Pasqua	IT	£3.00-3.50
Somerfield Beaujolais Dupond	FR	£3.50-4.00
Mâcon Rouge, G. Desire	FR	£4.50-5.00

- **Medium-bodied wines to serve on their own or with food**

Domaine de St-Julien VdP de l'Hérault	FR	£2.50-3.00
Somerfield Côtes-du-Rhône Celliers de l'Enclave des Papes	FR	£2.50-3.00
Leziria Vino de Mesa Tinto	P	£2.50-3.00
Somerfield Claret	FR	£3.00-3.50
Fitou	FR	£3.00-3.50
Somerfield Claret Eschenauer	FR	£3.00-3.50
Somerfield Syrah VdP d'Oc JeanJean	FR	£3.00-3.50
Chianti Conti Serristori	IT	£3.00-3.50
Cape Selection Pinotage	SA	£3.00-3.50
St Tropez Côtes de Provences	FR	£3.50-4.00
Copertino Puglia	IT	£3.50-4.00
Stambolovo Reserve Merlot	BU	£3.50-4.00
Château de Caraguilhes Corbières (*organic*)	FR	£4.00-4.50
Château la Rocheraie Bordeaux Supérieur	FR	£4.00-4.50*
Berberana Tempranillo Rioja	SP	£4.00-4.50

- **Heavier wines to serve with food**

Don Hugo Vino Tinto	SP	£2.50-3.00
Somerfiled Chilean Cabernet Sauvignon	CH	£3.00-3.50
Somerfield Rioja Tinto Crianza	SP	£3.50-4.00*
Somerfield Australian Cabernet Sauvignon	OZ	£3.50-4.00
Penfolds Cabernet Shiraz	OZ	£4.00-4.50

- **Good wines for parties**

Lesiria Tinto Cooperativa da Almeirim	P	£2.50-3.00

Somerfield VdP des Côtes de		
Gascogne	FR	£2.50-3.00
St Chinian	FR	£2.50-3.00*

- *Splashing out*

Senorio de Agos Rioja Reserva	SP	£5.00-5.50

Spar

The wines listed below are available to all Spar outlets. However individual managers have the authority to buy elsewhere and not all shops stock all these wines.

WHITE

- *Fresh and light wines for easy drinking at any time*

Spar La Mancha	SP	②	£2.50-3.00
VdP de l'Aude	FR	②	£3.00-3.50
Spar Muscadet de Sèvre-et-Maine	FR	①	£3.50-4.00*
Côtes de St Mont Tuiliere du Bosc	FR	②	£4.00-4.50*
Spar Frascati Superiore	IT	②	£4.00-4.50

Sauvignon Blanc and Sauvignon-based wines

Domaines des Fontanelles Sauvignon VdP			
d'Oc	FR	①	£3.50-4.00*

- *Fuller-flavoured and fruity, but still relatively dry, wines*

Riesling d'Alsace Turckheim	FR	②	£4.00-4.50

Chardonnay and Chardonnay blends

Chardonnay VdP d'Oc	FR	②	£3.50-4.00*
Hardy's Stamp Series Semillon/			
Chardonnay	OZ	②	£3.50-4.00
Glenn Ellen Chardonnay			
(particularly fruity)	USA	②	£4.00-4.50*

Jacob's Creek Chardonnay	OZ	③	£4.00-4.50
Henry Lindemans Semillon/			
Chardonnay	OZ	②	£4.00-4.50
Lindemans Bin 65 Chardonnay	OZ	②	£4.50-5.00

- ### *Medium dry, very fruity, wines to serve at any time*

Spar Hock	GER	④	£2.50-3.00
Piesporter Michelsberg	GER	④	£3.00-3.50
Deutscher Tafelwein Mosel	GER	④	£3.00-3.50

- ### *Sparkling wines for aperitifs and parties*

Spar Asti	IT	⑦	£5.00-5.50
Saumur Rosé Gratien Meyer	FR	①	£6.00-6.50
Orlando Carrington Extra Brut	OZ	①	£6.00-6.50
Crémant de Loire Gratien Meyer	FR	②	£6.50-7.00

- ### *Good wine for parties*

| Spar Valencia (Dry or Medium) | SP | ② | £2.50-3.00 |

- ### *Splashing out*

Cuvée d'Alban Bordeaux Blanc			
Dulong	FR	①	£5.50-6.00*
Chablis La Chablisiénne	FR	①	£7.50-8.00

RED

- ### *Light and fruity wines for easy drinking at any time*

VdP de l'Aude	FR		£2.50-3.00
VdP de la Cite de Carcassone	FR		£2.50-3.00
Domaine Montariol Syrah VdP			
d'Oc *(particularly fruity)*	FR		£3.00-3.50
Spar Merlot VdP d'Oc	FR		£3.00-3.50*

Spar La Mancha	SP	£3.00-3.50
Frankovka	CZ	£3.00-3.50
Viticoltori deli Acquese Barbera d'Asti	IT	£3.50-4.00*

- *Medium-bodied wines to serve on their own or with food*

Spar Côtes-du-Rhône	FR	£3.00-3.50
Spar VdP de l'Hérault	FR	£3.50-4.00
Spar Rioja	SP	£3.50-4.00
Spar Chianti	IT	£3.50-4.00

Cabernet Sauvignon and Cabernet blends

Spar Cabernet Sauvignon VdP de L'Aude	FR	£2.50-3.00
Cabernet Sauvignon & Cinsault Russe Region *(particularly fruity)*	BU	£2.50-3.00
Spar Claret Bordeaux Rouge	FR	£3.00-3.50
Korten Cabinet Sauvignon	BU	£3.00-3.50*
Glen Ellen Cabernet Sauvignon	USA	£4.50-5.00

- *Heavier wines to serve with food*

Jacob's Creek Dry Red	OZ	£4.00-4.50
Montepulciano d'Abruzzo	IT	£4.50-5.00
Errazuriz Panquehue Merlot	CH	£4.50-5.00*

Cabernet Sauvignon and Cabernet blends

Hardy's Stamp Series Cabernet Sauvignon *(particularly fruity)*	OZ	£3.50-4.00
Lindemans Cabernet/Shiraz	OZ	£4.00-4.50*
Lindemans Bin 45 Cabernet Sauvignon	OZ	£4.50-5.00

- *Good wines for parties*

Spar Valencia	SP	£2.50-3.00
Spar Cabernet Sauvignon and Merlot Pomorie	BU	£2.50-3.00

- **Splashing out**

Chianti Classico La Canonica	IT	Ⓒ	£5.00-5.50
Cook's Hawks Bay Cabernet Sauvignon	OZ	Ⓓ	£5.00-5.50

WHITE

- *Fresh and light wines for easy drinking at any time*

Tesco Escoubes VdP des Côtes de Gascogne *(particularly fruity)*	FR	②	£2.50-3.00*
Tesco Colli Lanuvini	IT	①	£2.50-3.00
Tesco Dry Hock	GER	①	£2.50-3.00
Cinco Casas La Mancha	SP	②	£2.50-3.00
Delta Domaines Cépages Terret VdP de l'Hérault *(distinctive)*	FR	②	£3.00-3.50
Tesco Pinot Grigio Del Veneto *(easy drinking)*	IT	①	£3.00-3.50
Tesco Baden Dry *(distinctive)*	GER	②	£3.00-3.50
Tesco Dry Vinho Verde	P	①	£3.00-3.50
Tesco White Bairrada	P	②	£3.00-3.50
Tesco Cape Chenin Blanc	SA	②	£3.00-3.50
Winzerhaus Pinot Blanc *(particularly fruity)*	A	③	£3.50-4.00

  Sauvignon Blanc and Sauvignon blends

Tesco Chilean White *(particularly fruity)*	CH	①	£2.50-3.00
Tesco Sauvignon Blanc Bordeaux	FR	①	£3.00-3.50
Tesco Swartland Sauvignon Blanc	SA	①	£3.50-4.00*
Tesco New Zealand Sauvignon Blanc	NZ	②	£4.00-4.50*

Fuller-flavoured and fruity, but still relatively dry, wines

Tesco Cape Colombar	SA	①	£2.50-3.00
Tesco Australian White, Rhine Riesling *(particularly fruity)*	OZ	②	£3.00-3.50*
Tesco White Rioja	SP	②	£3.50-4.00
Uvas del Sol Argentinian Torrentes *(distinctive)*	AR	②	£3.50-4.00
Tesco New Zealand Dry White	NZ	②	£3.50-4.00
Wildflower Ridge Chenin Blanc	OZ	③	£4.50-5.00*

Chardonnay and Chardonnay blends

Bulgarian Vintage Blend Chardonnay/Aligote	BU	②	£2.50-3.00
Tesco Australian Colombard/ Chardonnay *(distinctive)*	OZ	②	£3.50-4.00
Barramundi Semillon/Chardonnay	OZ	②	£3.50-4.00*
Tesco Robertson Chardonnay *(lightly oaky fruit)*	SA	②	£3.50-4.00*
Tesco les Domaine de St Pierre Chardonnay *(distinctive)*	FR	②	£4.00-4.50
Tesco Chilean Chardonnay/Semillon	CH	②	£4.00-4.50*
Hardy's Nottage Hill Chardonnay	OZ	②	£4.00-4.50*

Medium dry, very fruity, wines to serve at any time

Tesco Bernkasteler Kurfurstlay Riesling	GER	④	£3.00-3.50
Mosel Medium Dry Riesling	GER	③	£3.00-3.50
Tesco Orvieto Classico Abboccato	IT	④	£3.50-4.00
Domaine de la Jalousie Late Harvest Grassa	FR	④	£4.50-5.00*

Sparkling wines for aperitifs and parties

Tesco Asti	IT	⑦	£4.50-5.00
Sparkling Chardonnay	IT	②	£4.50-5.00
Tesco Australian Sparkling	OZ	①	£4.50-5.00
Tesco Sparkling Sauvignon Blanc Bergkelder	SA	①	£5.00-5.50

Sparkling Soave	IT	②	£5.50-6.00
Angas Brut Rosé	OZ	②	£6.00-6.50
Tesco Crémant de Bourgogne	FR	①	£7.00-7.50
Blue Ridge Brut	SA	②	£7.00-7.50

- **Dessert or pudding wines**

Tesco Moscatel de Valencia	SP	⑧	£3.00-3.50*
Muscat Cuvée Jose Sala	FR	⑧	£3.50-4.00*
Tesco Steinweiler Kloster Liefrauenberg Auslese	GER	⑦	£4.50-5.00*

- **Good wines for parties**

Tesco Bulgarian Country White *(easy drinking)*	BU	③	£2.50-3.00
Tesco Domaine St Alain VdP des Côtes du Tarn	FR	②	£3.00-3.50
Tesco Blayais Blanc	FR	②	£3.00-3.50

- **Splashing out**

Danie de Wet Chardonnay	SA	②	£5.00-5.50*
Grans Fassian Riesling Trocken	GER	②	£5.50-6.00

RED AND ROSÉ

- **Light and fruity wines for easy drinking at any time**

Tesco VdP des Bouches du Rhône *(easy drinking)*	FR	£2.50-3.00*
Dorgan VdP de l'Aude	FR	£2.50-3.00
Tesco VdP de l'Aude *(easy drinking)*	FR	£2.50-3.00
Tesco Gamay VdP du Jardin de la France	FR	£2.50-3.00
Tesco Sicilian Red	IT	£2.50-3.00
VdP de la Cite de Carcassonne	FR	£3.00-3.50
Tesco Domaine de Beaufort Minervois	FR	£3.00-3.50*

| Tesco Merlot del Piave | IT | £3.00-3.50 |
| Tesco Cabernet de Saumur Rosé | FR ② | £3.50-4.00 |

• *Medium-bodied wines to serve on their own or with food*

Tesco VdP des Côtes de Perignan		
(easy drinking)	FR	£2.50-3.00
Tesco Rosso del Salento *(distinctive)*	IT	£2.50-3.00
Don Darias	SP	£2.50-3.00
Marquis de Chive Tempranillo		
(oaky)	SP	£2.50-3.00
Quinta da Cardiga Ribatejo	P	£2.50-3.00
Grand Carat VdP du Comte Tolosan	FR	£3.00-3.50
Tesco Rosso el Lazio	IT	£3.00-3.50
Tesco Bairrada	P	£3.00-3.50
Uvas del Sol Argentinian Red		
(easy drinking)	AR	£3.00-3.50
Tesco Côtes-du-Rhône Villages	FR	£3.50-4.00
Domaine de la Source Syrah VdP		
de l'Hérault *(particularly fruity)*	FR	£3.50-4.00 *
Tesco Rosso del Piemonte	IT	£3.50-4.00*
Tesco Chilean Merlot Maipo Valley	CH	£4.00-4.50

Cabernet Sauvignon and Cabernet blends

Tesco Claret	FR	£3.00-3.50*
Tesco Cabernet del Veneto	IT	£3.00-3.50*
Château les Valentines Bergerac	FR	£4.00-4.50*
Tesco New Zealand Cabernet/		
Merlot	NZ	£4.00-4.50

• *Heavier wines to serve with food*

Tesco Chilean Red *(particularly*		
fruity)	CH	£2.50-3.00
Tesco Bairrada Red	P	£3.00-3.50
Borba Alentejo	P	£3.00-3.50
Tesco Douro	P	£3.00-3.50*
Casal Giglio Shiraz *(particularly*		
fruity)	IT	£3.50-4.00*

| Barramundi Shiraz/Merlot | OZ | £3.50-4.00 |
| Tesco Australian Shiraz, McLaren Vale | OZ | £4.00-4.50* |

Cabernet Sauvignon and Cabernet blends

Tesco Australian Red Shiraz/ Cabernert South Eastern Australia *(particularly fruity)*	OZ	£3.00-3.50*
Tesco South Australian Shiraz/ Cabernet	OZ	£3.50-4.00
Tesco South African Cabernet Sauvignon	SA	£4.00-4.50
Oak Village Vintage Reserve	SA	£4.00-4.50

• *Good wines for parties*

Tesco VdP des Côtes de Gascogne Rouge *(easy drinking)*	FR	£2.50-3.00
Tesco Bulgarian Country Red *(easy drinking)*	BU	£2.50-3.00
Tesco Hungarian Merlot *(particularly fruity and easy drinking)*	HU	£2.50-3.00
Tesco French Country Red VdP de l'Aude *(litre)*	FR	£3.50-4.00

• *Splashing out*

| Bourgueil la Hurolaie, Caslot-Galbrun | FR | £5.00-5.50 |
| Tesco Yarra Glen Pinot Noir | OZ | £6.00-6.50* |

WHITE

- *Fresh and light wines for easy drinking at any time*
  VdP des Côtes de Gascogne
    Domaine le Puts — FR ② £3.50-4.00*
  Muscadet de Sevre-et-Maine
    Château la Forchetière — FR ① £4.00-4.50
  Château Bauduc Entre-deux-Mers — FR ② £4.00-4.50
  Château de Haut Pomatede Graves — FR ② £4.00-4.50
  Torres Viña Sol Penedès — SP ① £4.50-5.00

  Sauvignon Blanc and Sauvignon-based wines
  Sauvignon de Haut Poitou — FR ① £4.00-4.50
  Sauvignon Trois Mouline — FR ① £4.00-4.50
  Sauvignon Blanc KWV — SA ① £4.00-4.50

- *Fuller-flavoured and fruity, but still relatively dry, wines*
  Peatlings Semillon/Colombard — OZ ① £4.00-4.50*

  Chardonnay and Chardonnay blends
  Khan Krum Chardonnay — BU ② £4.00-4.50
  Chardonnay Veneto del Colle Vino
    da Tavola — IT ② £4.00-4.50
  Peatlings Chardonnay — OZ ② £4.50-5.00
  Roos Leap Vineyards Chardonnay — OZ ② £4.50-5.00

- *Medium dry, very fruity, wines to serve at any time*
  Peatling's Niersteiner Gütes
    Domthal — GER ④ £3.00-3.50

- *Sparkling wines for aperitifs and parties*
  Piemontello Vino Frizzante — IT ⑤ £3.50-4.00

| Moscato Italvini | IT | ⑦ | £4.00-4.50 |
| Peatling's Sparkling Vin Mousseux Methode Traditionelle | FR | ① | £5.50-6.00 |

- *Dessert or pudding wine*
  | Peatling's Dry Fino Garvey | SP | ① | £4.50-5.00 |

- *Good wine for parties*
  | VdP de Terroirs Landais Domaine de Laballe | FR | ② | £3.00-3.50 |

- *Splashing out*
Peatling SE Australian Chardonnay	OZ	②	£5.00-5.00
Micheltons Marsanne	OZ	②	£7.00-7.50*
Jamiesons Run Chardonnay	OZ	②	£7.00-7.50

RED

- *Light and fruity wines for easy drinking at any time*
Sliven Merlot and Pinot Noir Country Wine	BU	£3.00-3.50
Côtes du Ventoux	FR	£3.00-3.50
VdP de Vaucluse	FR	£3.00-3.50

- *Medium-bodied wines to serve on their own or with food*
Peatling Côtes de Rousillon Villages	FR	£3.00-3.50
Peatling Corbières	FR	£3.00-3.50
Peatling's Mature Claret	FR	£4.00-4.50
Santa Helena Giglio de Oro Merlot	CH	£4.00-4.50
Stambulovo Merlot Reserve	BU	£4.00-4.50

  Cabernet Sauvignon and Cabernet blends
  | Oriachovitza Cabernet Sauvignon | BU | £4.00-4.50 |
  | Château Gassiot Côtes de Bourg | FR | £4.50-5.00 |

- *Heavier wines to serve with food*

Periquita Fonseca	P	£4.00-4.50
Torres Coronas	SP	£4.50-5.00

Cabernet Sauvignon and Cabernet blends

Peatling's Shiraz/Cabernet	OZ	£3.50-4.00
Thos. Peatling Cabernet Sauvingon		
VdP d'Oc	FR	£4.00-4.50

- *Good wines for parties*

Coteaux du Languedoc Château		
Flaugergues	FR	£3.00-3.50
Sliven Merlot and Pinot Noir	BU	£3.00-3.50

- *Splashing out*

Château Pitray Bordeaux Supérieur	FR	£5.00-5.50*
Beron Rioja	SP	£5.00-5.50
Cabernet Sauvignon Miguel Torres	SP	£5.00-5.50

Thresher

Both Bottoms Up and Wine Rack are part of the same group as Thresher. All three shops have many wines in common. However, you may find some wines in Bottoms Up and Wine Rack which are not stocked in Thresher. If you cannot find one of the wines listed below in your local Thresher ask the staff to direct you to the nearest Wine Rack or Bottoms Up.

WHITE

- *Fresh and light wines for easy drinking at any time*

   VdP des Côtes de Thau Les Acacias FR ① £2.50-3.00

Vega Camelia Rioja	SP	①	£3.00-3.50
Boland Colombard Paarl *(distinctive)*	SA	②	£3.00-3.50
Santara White Conca de Berbera	SP	②	£3.00-3.50
Domaine du Tariquet VdP des			
Côtes de Gascogne	FR	②	£3.50-4.00*
Bordeaux Sec Jean Paul Bartier	FR	①	£3.00-3.50
Château de la Rouergue			
Entre-deux-Mers *(particularly*			
fruity)	FR	②	£4.00-4.50

Sauvignon Blanc and Sauvignon-based wines

Moldova Sauvignon Blanc Ryman	M	①	£3.00-3.50
Villa Montes Sauvignon Blanc			
Ryman	CH	①	£3.50-4.00
Sauvignon Domaine des Salices			
VdP d'Oc *(particularly fruity)*	FR	①	£4.00-4.50*

• *Fuller-flavoured and fruity, but still relatively dry, wines*

Hungarian Muscat *(distinctively*			
fruity)	HU	②	£3.00-3.50*
Irsay Oliver Gyongyos Region			
(distinctively fruity)	HU		£3.00-3.50
Winelands Chenin Blanc *(easy*			
drinking)	SA	③	£3.00-3.50
Tollana Dry White	OZ	②	£3.00-3.50
Winelands Chenin Blanc			
(particularly fruity)	SA	②	£3.00-3.50
Winelands Muscat d'Alexandrie			
(distinctively fruity)	SA	③	£3.00-3.50*
Viña Las Gruesas *(distinctive)*	SP	②	£3.50-4.00*
Tollana Coonawarra Riesling	OZ	③	£3.50-4.00
Agramont Blanco Navarra *(oaky)*	SP	③	£4.50-.500

Chardonnay and Chardonnay blends

Chardonnay VdP d'Oc	FR	②	£3.00-3.50
Moldova Chardonnay Ryman			
(particularly fruity)	MO	②	£3.00-3.50*

Reserve Chardonnay Khan Krum	BU	②	£3.50-4.00
Le Cordon Lot 39 VdP d'Oc			
(particularly fruity)	FR	②	£3.50-4.00
Tollana Colombard/Chardonnay			
(particularly fruity)	OZ	②	£4.00-4.50*
Santa Carolina Chardonnay *(oaky)*	CH	②	£4.00-4.50

Medium dry, very fruity, wines to serve at any time

Bulgarian Muscat/Ugni Blanc			
Bourgas *(easy drinking)*	BU	④	£2.50-3.00
Bereich Bernkastel	GER	④	£3.00-3.50
Winelands Medium Dry			
(easy-drinking)	SA	④	£3.50-4.00

Sparkling wines for aperitifs and parties

Castellblanch Extra Brut	SP	①	£5.00-5.50
Seppelt Great Western Brut	OZ	①	£5.00-5.50*
Segura Viudas Brut Reserva	SP	②	£6.50-7.00*
Lindauer Brut	NZ	②	£7.00-7.50
Seaview Pinot/Chardonnay			
McLaren	OZ	②	£7.50-8.00*

Dessert or pudding wines

Muscat Petits Grains VdP des			
Collines de la Moure *(distinctively*			
fruity)	FR	⑦	£3.00-3.50*

Good wines for parties

Blanc de Blancs Vin de Table			
(easy drinking)	FR	②	£3.00-3.50
VdP de Gers Au Loubet *(particularly*			
fruity)	FR	②	£3.00-3.50*
Las Colinas Predro *(easy drinking)*	CH	②	£3.00-3.50

- **Splashing out**

Penfolds Koonunga Hill Chardonnay	OZ	②	£5.00-5.50*
Villiera Sauvignon Blanc *(particularly fruity)*	SA	①	£5.50-6.00
De Wetshof Rhine Riesling Robertson	SA	③	£6.00-6.50*

RED AND ROSÉ

- **Light and fruity wines for easy drinking at any time**

La Mission Côtes de Ventoux *(easy drinking)*	FR		£2.50-3.00
Campagnard VdP de l'Aude	FR		£3.00-3.50
Valpolicella	IT		£3.00-3.50
Santara Red Conca de Barbera *(easy drinking)*	SP		£3.00-3.50*
Bulgarian Vintage Blend Merlot/Pamid *(easy drinking)*	BU		£3.00-3.50*
Bulgarian Vintage Premier Merlot Iambol Region *(easy drinking)*	BU		£3.00-3.50
Boland Dry Red *(easy drinking)*	SA		£3.00-3.50
Romanian Pinot Noir	RO		£3.00-3.50*
Domaine de Grange Neuve Rosé Coteaux de Murviel	FR	②	£3.50-4.00*
Barbera d'Asti Viticoltori dell'Acquese	IT		£3.50-4.00
Château de Laurens Faugères *(easy drinking)*	FR		£4.00-4.50

- **Medium-bodied wines to serve on their own or with food**

Vega Camelia Rioja *(distinctive)*	SP	£3.00-3.50*

Tollana Red South Eastern Australia	OZ	£3.00-3.50
Figaro VdP l'Hérault	FR	£3.50-4.00
Rosso Piceno Umani Ronchi Marche	IT	£3.50-4.00
Quinta de Lamelas Douro (*particularly fruity*)	P	£3.50-4.00
Winelands Cinsault/Tinta Barocca	SA	£3.50-4.00
Le Cordon Lot 37 VdP d'Oc (*particularly fruity*)	FR	£4.00-4.50
Domaine les Colombies Corbières	FR	£4.00-4.50*
Domaine Ste Eulalie Minervois (*particularly fruity*)	FR	£4.00-4.50*

Cabernet Sauvignon and Cabernet blends

Country Red Cabernet Sauvignon/ Merlot Suhindol (*easy drinking*)	BU	£2.50-3.00
Bulgarian Vintage Premier Cabernet Sauvignon Iambol (*particularly fruity*)	BU	£3.00-3.50*
Bulgarian Vintage Blend Cabernet/ Merlot	BU	£3.00-3.50
Monte Ory Navarra (*particularly fruity*)	SP	£3.50-4.00
Las Colinas Merlot/Cabernet Santa Rosa (*particularly fruity*)	CH	£3.50-4.00
Domaine de Rivoyre Cabernet Sauvignon VdP d'Oc	FR	£4.00-4.50
Château Guibon Bordeaux (*particularly fruity*)	FR	£4.50-5.00

Heavier wines to serve with food

Alandra Herdade de Esporao Alentejo	P	£3.00-3.50
Berloup St Chinian	FR	£3.50-4.00
Chevite Reserve Navarro (*particularly fruity*)		£4.50-5.00

Cabernet Sauvignon and Cabernet blends

Tollana Shiraz/Cabernet	OZ	£4.00-4.50*

- *Good wines for parties*

Butlers Blend Country Wine		
Kekfrankos/Merlot Villany		
(easy drinking)	HU	£2.50-3.00
VdP des Coteaux de Peyriac		
(easy drinking)	FR	£2.50-3.00
Las Colina San Pedro *(easy drinking)*	CH	£2.50-3.00

- *Splashing out*

Château de Lastours Corbières	FR	£5.00-5.50*
Campo Viejo Rioja	SP	£5.00-5.50
Tollana Black Label Cabernet		
Sauvignon	OZ	£5.00-5.50*

Unwins

WHITE

- *Fresh and light wines for easy drinking at any time*

Bianco di Custoza	IT	②	£3.00-3.50
Muscadet de Sèvre-et-Maine	FR	①	£3.50-4.00
VdP des Côtes de Gascogne Grassa			
(particularly fruity)	FR	②	£3.50-4.00
Pinot Grigio del Veneto	IT	②	£3.50-4.00

Sauvignon Blanc and Sauvignon-based wines

Sauvignon Touraine	FR	①	£3.00-3.50
Sauvignon Bordeaux	FR	①	£3.50-4.00
Gyongyos Sauvignon Blanc	HU	①	£3.50-4.00

- *Fuller-flavoured and fruity, but still relatively dry, wines*

Penfolds Stockman's Bridge	OZ	②	£3.50-4.00
Chenin Blanc KWV	SA	④	£3.50-4.00

Chardonnary and Chardonnay blends

Domaine Collin Rosier VdP d'Oc			
Chardonnay	FR	②	£3.50-4.00
Gyongyos Chardonnay	HU	②	£3.50-4.00
Chardonnay Reserve Varna Region	BU	②	£3.50-4.00
Jacob's Creek Semillon/			
Chardonnay	OZ	②	£4.00-4.50

- *Medium dry, very fruity, wines to serve at any time*

Lamberhurst Sovereign	E	④	£2.50-3.00
Mainzer Domherr Kabinett	GER	④	£3.50-4.00

- *Sparkling wines for aperitifs and parties*

Carrington Extra Brut	OZ	②	£5.00-5.50
Varichon et Clerc Cates Blanche			
Blanc de Blanc Brut	FR	②	£6.00-6.50
Angas Brut Rosé	OZ	②	£6.00-6.50
Clairette de Die	FR	④	£6.50-7.00
Asti Martini	IT	⑦	£6.50-7.00
Seaview Pinot/Chardonnay	OZ	②	£7.00-7.50*
Lindauer Brut	NZ	②	£7.50-8.00

- *Good wines for parties*

Deinhard Vintage	GER	③	£2.50-3.00
Country Wine Muskat & Ugni Blanc			
(easy drinking)	BU	③	£2.50-3.00

- *Splashing out*

Montana Sauvignon Blanc	NZ	②	£5.50-6.00
Penfolds Koonumga Hill			
Chardonnay	OZ	②	£5.50-6.00

RED AND ROSÉ

- **Light and fruity wines for easy drinking at any time**

  Domaine St Denis VdP d'Oc

Cabernet Sauvignon *(easy drinking)*	FR	£3.00-3.50
Côtes du Rousillon *(very fruity)*	FR	£3.00-3.50*
Rosé d'Anjou	FR ③	£3.00-3.50
VdP des Côtes de Gascogne Michel de l'Enclos *(particularly fruity)*	FR	£3.00-3.50*
Valpolicella Classico	IT	£3.50-4.00
Weinviertel Blauer Zweigelt	A	£4.00-4.50
Concha y Toro Merlot	CH	£4.50-5.00*

- **Medium-bodied wines to serve on their own or with food**

Minervois	FR	£3.00-3.50*
Côtes du Fontonnais	FR	£3.50-4.00
Fitou Producteurs de Mont Tauch	FR	£3.50-4.00

  Cabernet Sauvignon and Cabernet blends

Country Wine Cabernet Sauvignon and Merlot Pavlikeni	BU	£2.50-3.00
Cabernet Sauvignon Villandry Region	HU	£2.50-3.00
Penfold's Stockman's Bridge	OZ	£3.50-4.00
Cabernet Sauvignon KWV	SA	£4.00-4.50

- **Heavier wines to serve with food**

Borba Adega	P	£4.00-4.50
Faustino Rivero Ulecia Rioja *(distinctive)*	SP	£4.50-5.00*

  Cabernet Sauvignon and Cabernet blends

Jacob's Creek Shiraz/Cabernet	OZ	£4.00-4.50
Tollana Shiraz Cabernet *(particularly fruity)*	OZ	£4.00-4.50

| Undurraga Cabernet Sauvignon | CH | £4.50-5.00 |

- *Good wines for parties*

| Castillo de Liria Valencia *(easy drinking)* | SP | £2.50-3.00 |
| Haskovo Merlot | BU | £3.00-3.50 |

- *Splashing out*

| Torres Coronas | SP | £5.00-5.50 |

The Victoria Wine Company

This chain of off-licence shops has bought the Augustus Barnett chain and the two are to be merged under the following trading names: Victoria Wine Cellars and Victoria Wine Stores. All the wines listed below can be ordered by the single bottle from any shop if they are not in stock.

WHITE

- *Fresh and light wines for easy drinking at any time*

Victoria Wine French Dry White VdP de l'Hérault	FR	②	£2.50-3.00
Castillo de Liria Valencia	SP	②	£2.50-3.00
Domaine l'Argentier Terret VdP Côtes de Thau *(distinctive)*	FR	②	£3.00-3.50
Domaine du Biau VdP des Côtes de Gascogne	FR	①	£3.00-3.50*
Soave Pasqua	IT	②	£3.00-3.50

Bianco di Custoza	IT	③	£3.00-3.50
Servus Bergenland *(easy drinking)*	AU	③	£3.00-3.50
Pinot Blanc Nagyrede	HU	②	£3.00-3.50
Corbières Blanc	FR	②	£3.50-4.00
Gaillac Blanc	FR	①	£3.50-4.00
Angelico Calvet *(easy drinking)*	FR	②	£3.50-4.00

Sauvignon Blanc and Sauvignon blends

La Serre Sauvignon Blanc VdP d'Oc	FR	①	£4.00-4.50*
Caliterra Sauvignon Blanc *(particularly fruity)*	CH	②	£4.00-4.50*

- *Fuller-flavoured and fruity, but still relatively dry, wines*

Dry Muscat di Puglia Le Trulle *(distinctively fruity)*	IT	③	£3.00-3.50
Marquès de Vitoria Oaked White *(oaky)*	SP	②	£3.00-3.50
Chapel Hill Irsay Oliver *(distinctive)*	CZ	③	£3.00-3.50
Simonsvlei Chenin Blanc *(easy drinking)*	SA	②	£3.00-3.50
Muscat Sec Domaine Montrabech VdP d'Oc *(distinctively fruity)*	FR	①	£3.50-4.00*
Randall Bridge Dry White	OZ	②	£3.50-4.00
Neethlingshof Gewürztraminer *(distinctive)*	SA	③	£4.00-4.50

Chardonnay and Chardonnay blends

Oak Forest Chardonnay	HU	②	£3.00-3.50
Hardy's Semillon/Chardonnay	OZ	②	£3.50-4.00
Hardy's Nottage Hill Chardonnay	OZ	②	£4.00-4.50*
Deakin Estate Colombard/ Chardonnay	OZ	②	£4.00-4.50
Hardy Nottage Hill Chardonnay	OZ	②	£4.50-5.00*

- *Medium dry, very fruity, wines to serve at any time*

Russe Country /white Muskat & Ugni Blanc *(easy drinking)*	BU	④	£3.00-3.50
Kabinett Bornheimer Adelberg	GER	③	£3.00-3.50

Cape White	S	④	£3.00-3.50
Vouvray Papillon	FR	④	£4.50-5.00

• *Sparkling wines for aperitifs and parties*

Sparkling Liebfraumilch	GER	⑤	£4.00-4.50
Sparkling Chardonnay Barbero	IT	②	£5.00-5.50
Cava Coniusa Brut	SP	②	£5.00-5.50
Angas Brut Yalumba Rosé	OZ	②	£6.00-6.50
Asti Martini	IT	⑥	£6.50-7.00
Martini Brut	IT	②	£6.50-7.00
Codorniu Première Cuvée Brut	SP	②	£6.50-7.00
Lindauer Brut Montana	NZ	②	£7.00-7.50

• *Dessert or pudding wines*

Stellenzicht Noble Late Harvest Weisser Riesling *(distinctive) (half)*	SA	②	£3.50-4.00*

• *Good wines for parties*

VdP de Vaucluse Blanc La mission	FR	②	£2.50-3.00
Chapel Hill Hungarian Rhine Riesling	HU	①	£2.50-3.00
Hincesti Chardonnay *(particularly fruity)*	HU	②	£3.00-3.50*

• *Splashing out*

Moondah Brook Chenin Blanc	OZ	②	£4.50-5.00
Corbett Canyon Chardonnay *(oaky)*	OZ	②	£5.00-4.50*
Muscat Cuvée Tradition Turkheim Alsace	FR	②	£5.00-5.50*
Penfolds Koonunga Hill Chardonnay	OZ	②	£5.00-5.50*

RED AND ROSÉ

- *Light and fruity wines for easy drinking at any time*

VdP de Vaucluse	FR	£2.50-3.00
Victoria Wine VdP de l'Hérault	FR	£3.00-3.50
Rosso del Veneto	IT	£3.00-3.50
Cortenova Merlot Pasqua	IT	£3.00-3.50
Hungarian Merlot	HU	£3.00-3.50
Bear Ridge Gamza *(easy drinking)*	BU	£3.00-3.50
Baron Rocheau Côtes de Duras	FR	£3.50-4.00
Syrah Rosé Fortant de France VdP d'Oc	FR ③	£3.50-4.00
Teroldego Rotaliano	IT	£3.50-4.00
Rosso Conero Umani Ronchi	IT	£4.00-4.50

- *Medium-bodied wines to serve on their own or with food*

Sangiovese di Toscana Vino da Tavola	IT	£3.00-3.50*
Minervois Caves des Hautes Coteaux	FR	£3.50-4.00
Fitou Cuvée Mme C. Parmentier	FR	£3.50-4.00
Val de Sensac Côtes de St-Mont	FR	£4.00-4.50
Chianti Colli Senesi Castello di Montauto	IT	£4.00-4.50

Cabernet Sauvignon and Cabernet blends

Debut Cabernet Sauvignon *(particularly fruity)*	BU	£3.00-3.50*
Pavlikeni Cabernet Sauvignon & Merlot	BU	£3.00-3.50
Domaine de Rivoyre Cabernet Sauvigon VdP d'Oc	FR	£4.00-4.50

- *Heavier wines to serve with food*

Casa Barco Vino de Mesa Oaked Red *(oaky)*	SP	£2.50-3.00

Leziria Adega Co-op	P	£2.50-3.00
Borba	P	£3.50-4.00*
Rivarey Rioja	SP	£4.00-4.50
Quinta de Camarate Fonseca		
(*distinctive*)	P	£4.50-5.00
Chivite Reserva Navarra	SP	£4.50-5.00*

Cabernet Sauvignon and Cabernet blends

Hardy's Shiraz/Cabernet Stamp		
Series	OZ	£3.50-4.00
Woodford Hill Cabernet Sauvignon/		
Shiraz (*particularly fruity*)	OZ	£4.00-4.50*

- *Good wines for parties*

Hungarian Country Red Villany		
(*easy drinking*)	HU	£2.50-3.00*
Cabernet Sauvignon Szekzard		
(*easy drinking*)	HU	£3.00-3.50
Domaine St Laurent VdP des		
Coteaux du Libron	FR	£3.00-3.50

- *Splashing out*

Merlot Errazuriz Panquehue	CH	£5.00-5.50*
Campo Viejo Rioja (*particularly fruity*)	SP	£5.00-5.50
Croze Hermitage Gabriel Meffre	FR	£5.50-6.00
Garrafeira Fonsec (*particularly		
distinctive and fruity*)	P	£6.50-7.00*

Waitrose

WHITE

- *Fresh and light wines for easy drinking at any time*

| Blanc de Mer Vin de Tables | FR ① | £2.50-3.00 |

Le Pujalet VdP du Gers			
(particularly fruity)	FR	①	£2.50-3.00
Domaine de Planterieu VdP des			
Côtes de Gascogne	FR	②	£3.00-3.50
Terret VdP des Côtes de Thau			
Lurton *(distinctive)*	FR	②	£3.00-3.50
Waitrose Nuragus di Cagliari	IT	②	£3.00-3.50
Baden Dry Badischer Winzerkeller	GER	②	£3.00-3.50
Orvieto Classico Cardeto	IT	②	£3.50-4.00
Gruner Veltliner Lenz Moser	A	①	£4.00-4.50

Sauvignon Blanc and Sauvignon blends

Bordeaux Sauvignon Blanc	FR	①	£2.50-3.00
Domaine des Fontanelles Sauvignon			
VdP d'Oc	FR	①	£3.00-3.50
Château Darzac Entre-deux-Mers	FR	①	£4.00-4.50*
Touraine Sauvignon Domaine			
Gibault *(particularly fruity)*	FR	①	£4.00-4.50*
Château Haut Rian Bordeaux	FR	②	£4.00-4.50*

- *Fuller-flavoured and fruity, but still relatively dry, wines*

Don Hugo Blanco	SP	②	£2.50-3.00
Van Riebeeck Cape Dry White	SA	②	£2.50-3.00
Vilonds Muscat VdP de l'Hérault			
(distinctively fruity)	FR	②	£3.50-4.00
Penfolds Bin 202 Riesling	OZ	②	£3.50-4.00
Houghton Wild flower Ridge			
Chenin Blanc *(particularly fruity)*	OZ	②	£4.50-5.00*

Chardonnay and Chardonnay blends

Szeksard Chardonnay	HU	②	£3.00-3.50
Hardys Southern Creek			
Semillon/Chardonnay	OZ	③	£3.50-4.00
Currawong Creek Chardonnay	OZ	②	£3.50-4.00*
Hardys Nottage Hill Chardonnay			
(oaky)	OZ	②	£4.00-4.50*
Montenuevo Chardonnay	CH	②	£4.50-5.00*

• *Medium dry, very fruity, wines to serve at any time*

Waitrose Bereich Bernkastel	GER	④	£2.50-3.00
Priory, Lamberhurst Vineyards	E	③	£3.00-3.50
Waitrose Riesling Mosel Kabinett	GER	④	£3.00-3.50
Waitrose Piesporter Michelsberg	GER	④	£3.00-3.50

• *Sparkling wines for aperitifs and parties*

Seppelt Great Western Brut *(toasty)*	OZ	②	£4.50-5.00*
Castellblanch Cristal Brut Cava	SP	②	£5.00-5.50
Angas Brut Rosé	OZ	②	£5.50-6.00
Waitrose Saumur Brut	FR	①	£6.00-6.50*
Waitrose Blanquette de Limoux Brut	FR	①	£6.00-6.50

Chardonnay

Le Baron de Beaumont Chardonnay Brut	FR	②	£4.50-5.00
Santi Chardonnay Brut	IT	②	£5.00-5.50*
Crémant de Bourgogne Blanc Lugny *(particularly fruity)*	FR	②	£6.00-6.50*

• *Dessert or pudding wines*

Westofener Bergloster Auslese Pfalz *(particularly rich and fruity)*	GER	⑥	£4.00-4.50*

• *Good wines for parties*

Castillo de Liria Valencia	SP	②	£2.50-3.00
Waitrose Riesling	GER	③	£2.50-3.00
VdP du Jardin de la France	FR	②	£3.00-3.50

• *Splashing out*

Avontuur Chardonnay	SA	②	£5.00-5.50*
Brown Brothers King Valley Rhine Riesling *(particularly fruity)*	OZ	②	£6.00-6.50*
Pouilly Fumé Domaine Masson-Blondelet	FR	①	£6.00-6.50*

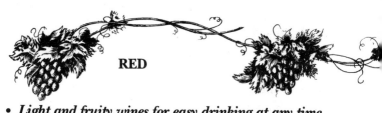

RED

- **Light and fruity wines for easy drinking at any time**

St Chinian	FR	£2.50-3.00*
Domaine des Fontaines Merlot VdP		
Pays d'Oc	FR	£3.00-3.50
Château Marseau Côtes du		
Marmandais	FR	£3.00-3.50
Minervois	FR	£3.00-3.50
Haut Poitou Gamay	FR	£3.50-4.00
Avontuur Cabernet Merlot		
Stellenbosch	SA	£3.50-4.00*
Château de la Roche Gamay		
Touraine *(particularly fruity)*	FR	£4.00-4.50
Moncenay Pinot Noir VdP de la		
Côte d'Or	FR	£4.00-4.50
Zinfandel Cartlidge & Browne	USA	£4.00-4.50*

- **Medium-bodied wines to serve on their own or with food**

Don Hugo Alto Ebro	SP	£2.50-3.00
Bergerac Rouge	FR	£2.50-3.00
Côtes de Duras Seigneuret	FR	£3.00-3.50
Waitrose Côtes-du-Rhône	FR	£3.00-3.50
Domaine de Beausejour Côtes de la		
Malepère	FR	£3.00-3.50*
Waitrose Monica di Sardegna		
Dolianova	IT	£3.00-3.50
Rosso Conero Umani Ronchi		
(distinctive)	IT	£3.50-4.00
Fitou	FR	£3.50-4.00
Château Senailhac Bordeaux	FR	£4.00-4.50*
Teroldego Rotaliano Gaierhof	IT	£4.00-4.50*

Cabernet Sauvignon and Cabernet blends

Cabernet Sauvignon Russe	BU	£2.50-3.00

Foncalieu Cabernet Sauvignon VdP de l'Aude	FR	£3.00-3.50*
Vintage Blend Cabernet Sauvignon & Merlot Iambol Region	BU	£3.00-3.50
Spring Gully Shiraz/Cabernet Sauvignon	OZ	£3.50-4.00
Cabernet Sauvignon VdP d'Oc	FR	£4.00-4.50*

Heavier wines to serve with food

Syrah VdP des Comtes Rhodaniens *(distinctive)*	FR	£3.00-3.50
Bairrada Dom Ferraz	P	£3.00-3.50
Culemborg Pinotage Paarl	SA	£3.00-3.50
Cahors Cuvée Reserve *(particularly heavy)*	FR	£3.50-4.00
Château St-Maurice Côtes de Rhône *(particularly fruity and distinctive)*	FR	£3.50-4.00
Concha y Toro Merlot *(particularly fruity)*	CH	£3.50-4.00
Château St-Maurice Côtes-du-Rhône *(particularly fruity and distinctive)*	FR	£3.50-4.00*
Rioja Cosme Palacio *(oaky)*	SP	£4.50-5.00*

Cabernet Sauvignon and Cabernet blends

Penfolds Bin 35 Shiraz/Cabernet	OZ	£4.00-4.50*

Good wines for parties

Ramada Vinho de Mesa Co-op de Almeiria *(particularly fruity)*	P	£2.00-2.50
Merlot/Pinot Noir Sliven	BU	£2.50-3.00
Le Secret VdP de Vaucluse *(very easy drinking)*	FR	£2.50-3.00
Château de Nages Costières de Nîmes	FR	£3.00-3.50

- *Splashing out*

  Montana Cabernet Sauvignon
     Marlborough   NZ   £5.00-5.50*
  Fetzer Valley Oaks Cabernet
     Sauvignon   USA   £5.50-6.00

Wine Rack

This chain of high street off-licences is now part of the Thresher Group and many of the same wines are stocked in both stores, though Wine Rack does stock some wines which do not appear on the shelves at Thresher. However, because of the size of the overlap I have listed all my recommendations for both stores under Thresher on page 107.

Wm Low

This store is about to be taken over by one of the major supermarket chains and the wine list is likely to change dramatically.

The French Option

All prices in this section are approximate. They are based on an exchange rate of eight francs to the pound.

Continent Calais

Situated North of Calais on the road to Dunkeurque.

WHITE

Good buys

Rosé de Loire	FR	②	£2.00-2.50
Muscadet de Sèvre-et-Maine, Caves de la Huchette	FR	①	£2.50.-3.00
Muscadet de Sèvre-et-Main Sur Lie Cave de Val & Mont	FR	①	£2.50-3.00
Jurançon Sec	FR	②	£3.50-4.00*
Clairette de Die *(sparkling)*	FR	⑤	£3.50-4.00
Gratien & Meyer Saumur Brut *(sparkling)*	FR	②	£4.00-4.50
St Germain Champagne	FR	①	£8.50-9.00*
Keller Champagne	FR	①	£8.50-9.00

Quite good

Saumur Blanc	FR	①	£2.00-2.50
Sauvignon Touraine	FR	①	£2.00-2.50
Blanquette de Limoux *(sparkling)*	FR	②	£3.00-3.50

RED

- ### *Good buys*

Château Vieux Ligat Côte de Bourg	FR	£1.50-2.00*
Les Grand Cailloux Cairanne,		
Côtes-du-Rhône Villages	FR	£2.50-3.00*
Château Haut Secondo Premières		
Côtes de Blaye	FR	£3.00-3.50
Marquès de Caceras Rioja	SP	£3.50-4.00*

- ### *Quite good*

Côtes de Bourg La Huchette	FR	£1.50-2.00
Château Le Trey Bordeaux	FR	£1.50-2.00
Côtes de Marmandais	FR	£2.00-2.50
Château Pevrenche Côtes de		
Castillon	FR	£2.50-3.00

- ### *Fair*

Château de Grand Caument		
Corbières	FR	£2.00-2.50
Château de Deuvre Vinsobres		
Côtes-du-Rhône Villages	FR	£3.00-3.50

Hyper Cedico

Situated on route N43 from Calais to St Omer, just outside Ardres. Tesco stores has an interest in this company and some of their wines are on the shelves.

WHITE

Good buys

VdP de l'Aude Blanc (Tesco)	FR	②	£1.50-2.00*
Dry Muscat VdP des Pyrenees Orientales (Tesco)	FR	②	£2.00-2.50
Touraine Sauvignon Sec La Follaine	FR	①	£2.00-2.50
Entre-deux-Mers (Tesco)	FR	②	£2.50-3.00
Dopff Riesling d'Alsace	FR	①	£3.50-4.00
Gratien & Meyer Saumur Brut (*sparkling*)	FR	②	£3.50-4.00
St Germain Champagne	FR	①	£10.50-11.00
Mercier Champagne	FR	①	£11.00-11.50

Quite good

Bergerac Blanc (Tesco)	FR	①	£2.00-2.50
Anjou Blanc (Tesco)	FR	②	£2.00-2.50

RED

Good buy

Touraine Gamay Ronsard	FR	£1.50-2.00*
Dorgon VdP de l'Aude (Tesco)	FR	£1.50-2.00*

VdP Côtes de Gascogne (Tesco)	FR	£2.00-2.50
Chinon Château de St Louande	FR	£2.50-3.00
Celliers du Dauphin Côtes-du-Rhône	FR	£2.00-2.50

- *Fair*

Château de la Banquière, Coteaux du Languedoc	FR	£1.50-2.00

Situated on route N43 to St Omer on the outskirts of Calais. Another branch is situated on the old road to Boulogne.

WHITE

- *Good buy*

Molières Cépage Muscat VdP de l'Hérault	FR	②	£1.50-2.00
Chardonnay VdP Jardin de la France	FR	②	£2.00-2.50
Château La Corerais-Cheneau Muscadet Sèvre-et-Maine Sur Lie	FR	①	£2.00-2.50
Château Haut Rian Entre-deux-Mers	FR	②	£2.50-3.00
Pinot d'Alsace	FR	②	£2.50-3.00
Château Flamand Graves	FR	②	£3.00-3.50
Muscadet Sur Lie Château de La Cassemichère	FR	①	£3.50-4.00
Mâcon Villages Bouchard	FR	②	£3.50-4.00

- *Quite good*

Château Mire L'Etang Cuvée Bois Coteaux de Languedoc	FR	②	£1.50-2.00

Bourgogne Chardonnay Bouchard
Père et Fils — FR ② £4.00-4.50

• *Fair*

Riesling d'Alsace Freyermuth — FR ② £3.00.3.50

RED

• *Good buys*

Caberent Sauvignon VdP Vallée de l'Aude (Tesco)	FR	£2.00-2.50*
Fitou (Tesco)	FR	£2.00-2.50
Julienas, Mommesan	FR	£3.50-4.00*

• *Quite good*

Corbières (Tesco)	FR	£1.50-2.00
Syrah VdP d'Oc (Tesco)	FR	£2.50-3.00

• *Fair*

Côtes du Ventoux Rosé Veille Caves du Fontange	FR	£1.00-1.50
Morgon, Mommesan	FR	£3.50-4.00

Mammoth

Situated on the old road to Boulogne from Calais.

WHITE

- **Good buys**

Mercier Champagne	FR	①	£10.00-10.50*
Lanson Brut Champagne	FR	①	£11.50-12.00*

- **Fair**

Pouilly Sur Loire	FR	①	£3.50-4.00

RED AND ROSÉ

- **Good buys**

Cabernet Sauvignon VdP d'Oc		
Raoul Lusing	FR	£1.50-2.00*
Bardolino Chiaretto (rosé)	IT	£2.00-2.50
Saumur La Turonne	FR	£2.50-3.00*
Carla de Plata Rioja Berberana	SP	£2.50-3.00*
Torres Sangredetoro	SP	£3.00-3.50
Errazuriz Cabernet Sauvignon	CH	£3.00-3.50

- **Quite good**

VdP de la Cite de Carcassonne	FR	£1.00-1.50*
Domaine Moulin Nouvel Minervois	FR	£1.50-2.00
Bourgeuil	FR	£3.50-4.00

Enjoying Wine

Wine and health

Wine, taken in moderation, is not harmful. Quite the contrary - it will probably do you some good. This statement is not nearly as startling as it used to be. More and more medical research, both in the US and in Europe, is pointing to the benefits of drinking alcohol and the doom and despondency generated by the anti-alcohol lobby is beginning to lift.

Even sceptical experts seem to agree that the moderate use of alcohol has a very strong cardio-protective effect. In plain language this means wine is good for your heart. People who drink in moderation also have the lowest death rate from most causes and the lowest overall mortality rate. This means that they are no more susceptible to accidents, cancer or suicide than non-drinkers. Drinking wine at table also has a beneficial effect on digestion.

Of course, alcohol taken in excess is extremely bad for you and there are small numbers of people who do abuse the use of alcohol.

So, what is moderate drinking? This is a difficult question to answer because levels of alcohol tolerance vary from one person to another. Body weight is important and lighter people, such as women, will not be able to tolerate as much as heavier people. Food is also important for absorption of alcohol takes a much shorter time on an empty stomach than on a full one. Metabolic rates are also relevant, which means that women can generally tolerate less than men, as their rates are naturally lower.

Many doctors in the UK have taken up the recommendations of the Royal College of Physicians which suggest that drinks should be divided up into units. Thus 1 unit equals a small measure of spirits, a glass of wine or half a pint of beer. Women are recommended to stick to 14 units a week and men to 21 units.

These recommendations do not have any scientific

background, but they are probably useful guidelines for levels of safe drinking. They are not sacrosanct limits beyond which you will inevitably turn into an alcoholic. Indeed the two-three glasses a day which these guidelines allow match the 'moderate' amounts outlined in the research.

In France they are much more liberal. French doctors work on body weight and offer 1 gram of alcohol per kilogram of body weight which means a person weighing 155 pounds can safely drink one bottle of wine a day. Timing is important here. If you decide to follow the French doctors, drink the bottle in stages, not all at once!

However, wine is quite high in calories. Average figures are around 90-95 kilocalories per glass of white wine and 95-100 for red wine. It is the alcohol in the wine that provides the calories. The sugar content is usually too small to make much difference. Thus, German wines, like Liebfraumilch, which are quite sweet but low in alcohol, contain fewer calories than drier wines, such as Chablis. Exceptions are Mateus Rosé and Asti Spumante, which really are very sweet.

Statistics on the consumption of alcohol are few and far between but what there are seem to show that consumption has remained relatively static for the last ten years. They also show that within the total, consumption among young men in the 18 to 24 age group (lager louts?) has fallen with women taking up the slack and drinking a little more.

So far, there have been very few research projects to either prove, or disprove, statements about the adverse effects of alcohol on absenteeism, crime and the like but the research quoted above does show that accidents are not an immediate consequence of drinking. Could it be that alcohol was being blamed for some of the general ills of the late twentieth century? After all a crime is reported as drink-related if anyone involved has had a single pint of beer within an hour or so of the crime.

Finally, it is comforting to know that cirrhosis of the liver, caused by alcohol alone, is now a rare complaint. We simply do not down the huge amounts of alcohol that some of our ancestors did. Like so many things, alcohol taken in excess is harmful. But, unlike some, taken in moderation it is beneficial.

Low and no-alcohol wines

There seems to be a ready market for wine which has had its alcohol content either removed or drastically reduced. **Tesco**, for example, currently offer 11 such wines. But can you really call it wine?

If all the alcohol has been removed from a wine it may indeed still legally be called wine. But if natural fermentation has taken place but has been stopped by some means or other when only a small amount of alcohol has been obtained from the grapes the result may not be called wine. This seems a little odd.

Odd, too, are the legal definitions. Alcohol-free wine should mean just that but in practice it means less than 0.05 per cent. Not a problem for most of us but it could conceivably be difficult for anyone with a strict dietary or cultural need to avoid all alcohol.

De-alcoholised describes the process a wine goes through but doe not mean that no alcohol is present. There is usually between 0.05 and 0.5 per cent alcohol still present.

Even more confusing are the phrases 'reduced alcohol' or 'low alcohol'. Neither of these descriptions has any accurate definition. The wine might contain anything from 0.5 to 5.5 per cent (normal wine being around 8-13 per cent).

If you are planning to buy one of these products it is obviously important to read the small print on the label where the actual alcoholic content is given. Remember that 'low alcohol wine' at 5.5 per cent contains more alcohol that some beers and lagers.

A while back the government announced that they were proposing to limit the use of the phrase 'low alcohol' to products containing less than 1.2 per cent alcohol. But the proposals have been shelved on the grounds that the EU is making its own proposals.

No and low-alcohol wines are obviously an attractive idea but are they an attractive buy? From a purely economic point of view the answer is yes. They are now cheaper than real wine. The excise duty that they used to attract has been lowered to rates more proportional to their alcohol content. Alcohol-free wines do not command any duty at all.

But what of the taste? Sadly these wines simply do not have the same aroma and flavour as real wine. A good deal is lost in the de-alcoholising process. The only wine I have tasted which comes anywhere near to the taste of real wine is Loxon low alcohol Chardonnay. It contains 1.2 per cent alcohol and is a surprisingly pleasant drink.

On the whole I would recommend anyone who wants to cut down on their alcohol intake to drink fewer (and maybe better?) glasses of wine or to add some sparkling water to the wind and revive the old custom of making spritzers. If you want to cut out alcohol altogether drink fruit juice.

The problem of flavour may be solved in time. Producers are spending thousands of pounds in research and millions of pounds in building bigger and better de-alcoholising plants. Current methods include arrested fermentation (usually producing wines with 2.5 to 5.5 per cent alcohol), heat treatment, centrifusion, reverse osmosis and dilution (usually with fruit juices).

This last method seems to be the most successful in the marketplace. The choice of so-called 'fruit' wines is expanding rapidly. They come in at anything from 3 per cent alcohol by volume to as much as 7.5 per cent. So once again it is important to read the label carefully. Flavours include raspberry, blackcurrant, banana, peach, tangerine and quite a few more.

If you want to experiment with no and low-alcohol wines try own-label or one of the following brands: Chiron, Eisberg, Escombes, Giocobuzzi, Golden Oktober, Masson, Pétillant de Listel, Sichel.

Rather better than most of these is **Majestic Wine Warehouses'** Electra Orange Muscat produced by Andrew Quady in California. This has an alcoholic level of 4 per cent by volume. It has a pleasant spritz and is not too cloyingly sweet. The Orange Muscat grape gives it a kind of Seville orange and apricot flavour which does not taste as artificial as some of the other low alcohol wines on the market.

Wine at home

If you like wine, there are numerous occasions for drinking it and there is no real reason why you shouldn't serve your favourite wines at any one of them. However, anything which is overworked becomes less interesting and boredom could creep in. It's much more fun to find a wide range of wines which are pleasing to you and to serve them at different occasions as you feel appropriate.

Your pocket will dictate some of the choices. You are more likely to serve a cheaper wine at a party where you are providing a dozen or more bottles and keep your more extravagant purchases for an intimate meal with friends or with your partner alone.

Party wines (for obvious reasons) should not be too high in alcohol or too definite. Your friends may not all appreciate your taste in oaky whites or tannic reds. Light Italian wines, French Vin de Pays and Penedès wines from Spain are good choices. The time of the year makes a difference, too. Heavy wines with a high alcohol content can be too much on a hot summer's evening, but very warming and festive at Christmas. But at the end of the day the choice is yours.

Opening wine

Start with a good corkscrew and most problems will be avoided. Choose one with a wide spiral that ends in a curved, not straight, point. A Brabantia or Screwpull are both excellent for all corks, but essential for long corks such as those used in fine wines and vintage port. A 'waiter's friend' (the type used by wine waiters) is good for everyday use. The double lever type is fine too, if it has a curved end.

There's no special skill in opening a bottle of wine, but you should either remove the capsule which covers the top of the neck altogether, or cut it round so that it is clear of the lip. This is particularly important if it is made of lead (increasingly rare). Some people like to leave the lower part of the capsule in place so that if the bottle touches the rim of the glass, the impact is softened.

Next wipe the top of the bottle with a damp cloth to remove any dirt or moulds (harmless) which have grown under the capsule. Insert the corkscrew and remove the cork. Wipe the rim again and pour.

Sometimes small pieces of cork will fall into the wine (curly-ended corkscrews keep this problem to a minimum) or the cork may even be so crumbly that it partially breaks up. This doesn't affect the wine. You can either pick out the pieces or sieve the wine into a flask or decanter.

Very occasionally corks are infected with a fungal growth which makes both the cork and the wine smell very mouldy. This is known as corked wine and it should not be drunk. Return the bottle and the cork to the shop where it was bought. There is no obligation to replace it, but reputable shops want to know if their wine is corked so that they can alert the original supplier and, nine times out of ten, they will replace the bottle for you.

Opening bottles of Champagne or sparkling wine does require a little more care and skill. Corks have been known to fly out the moment the pressure of the wire cage is removed and if the bottle is pointing at your face, or at other people, the result can be disastrous. So, keep a firm thumb on the top of the cork as you remove it and ease the cork out slowly and carefully. (There's no need to make a huge pop!) Keep the bottle pointing at the ceiling.

To decant or not?

None of the wine recommended in this book is likely to need decanting. Only fine clarets and vintage ports throw a sediment these days, all other wines are either too young to have developed any, or are so well filtered that even ten or twelve years in bottle does not produce any.

If you do buy or are given a fine claret or port, decant by very carefully pouring the wine from the bottle into the decanter in one continuous movement. Forget the candle and position a bright light behind the bottle so that you can see when the sediment reaches the neck. Stop pouring. Use the small amount of wine left in the bottle to enhance the gravy you are serving with the roast beef!

There are other reasons for decanting wines. You may have a fine glass decanter which you want to show off, or you may not want your guests to see the label or the bottle.

You may also want the air to get to the wine to allow it to take up the oxygen (breathe) and so age quickly. Test this for yourself by experimenting with a bottle of good Chianti. Try it when you open it, an hour after that, and then after another hour. Try it again the next day and you will see what happens to it. Remember to agitate the bottle before pouring as the top layer of liquid nearest to the air will oxidise before the rest.

Generally speaking, the younger the wine, the more it will benefit from a little air. This does not, however, apply to wines which do not have any ageing potential at all. So, don't try it with white wines, Vin de Pays, Valpolicella and the like.

The French, who have very definite ideas about these things, believe that the glass is decanter enough. If you think your wine needs improving after you pour it, you can deliberately aerate it by swishing it round the glass for a moment before you drink it.

Temperature control

Serve white wine at cellar temperature and red wine at room temperature. This is the traditional advice, but who has a wine cellar these days to check on the temperature? An hour in the fridge is probably more useful advice today. White wine should not be over-chilled. This is particularly important for those fresh, dry wines costing under £3.00 a bottle. There will be nothing to taste if they're too cold!

Room temperature creates another problem. In the days when there was no central heating, room temperature was lower than it is today! Red wine should be served at around 15°C, give or take a degree. So, check the temperature of the spare room and keep your bottles in there! If your wine is too cold, don't put it by the radiator - only one side will heat up (or overheat). Better to plunge the bottle into warm water for a very short time.

Some red wines, such as Beaujolais and Bardolino, are very good served chilled. Try it in summer.

Glasses

The glass you drink out of does affect your appreciation. Think of that good bottle of Chablis you drank out of the plastic mugs last summer. Did it taste the same as usual? So, don't just use any old glass. Simple Paris goblets are just about okay, but try using glasses where the shape of the upper space funnels slightly inwards. This channels the aroma and bouquet towards the nose and helps you to enjoy both the smell and the taste of the wine.

Don't give way to custom and fill the glass completely full. It is not mean to leave a space at the top of the glass - again to enjoy the aroma.

Sparkling wine is best served in slightly tall or fluted glasses to charm the bubble up in long attractive trails. Old-fashioned saucer-shaped glasses dissipate the bubbles and are easy to spill. They are best kept for ice-cream sundaes.

Short-term storage

If you haven't finished all the wine in the bottle, you can simply re-cork. Avoid the temptation to turn the cork upside down. It's easier to push back in this way, but you could be adding a cocktail of nasty bacteria or moulds. You might cut the end off first and then replace. Place the bottle in the fridge and drink the next day.

It's a better idea to invest in one of the proprietary bottle stoppers. Some are better than others, but people tend not to agree on which is which. I use the pump-out-air or vacuum-type and find it very satisfactory. But there are gas types as well.

If you have bought in wine for a party, store it in the coolest room in the house. Weekend stocks for the following week will be perfectly all right in the kitchen, but do lie the bottles on their sides to stop corks drying out.

Thinking about a cellar

The word 'cellar' may seem too grandiose a word to describe the space in which most of us keep surplus stocks of wine. But whatever its shape, size or location (even the kitchen), a stock of wine for future drinking is, indeed, a cellar.

It's quite sensible to buy in stocks of wine, even if you are paying less than £5.00 a bottle. First of all you have wines on hand to offer to unexpected visitors. You can also build up a selection of wine so that you have a choice of what to serve at a special dinner or at that evening cards session.

Even more importantly, quite a lot of wines improve with as little as six months or a year's extra bottle age. Phrases like 'still very young', 'full of promise' and 'will benefit if kept' appear in both supermarket and wine-shop literature and point the way. You could also save a little money by buying when you see first the wines. Prices could rise and you may not even be able to find the same vintage in a year or two.

Having bought yourself several bottles or even a case or two of wine you will need to store them. A wooden or wire rack is best, but cases of wine with proper compartments can just be turned on their sides and be used and re-used. Remember always to take the wine from the top first. The cardboard sections are rarely strong enough if unsupported by the bottle below.

If possible, keep your store of wine in the dark. the temperature is not critical provided that it does not change too rapidly from hot to cold or vice versa. If you do get temperature changes the wine will age more quickly. White wine may throw a sediment of crystals in very cold weather, but it only means that the wine has not been centrifuged to death and it won't affect the taste of the wine.

Most homes reveal one or two areas which can be pressed into service as a cellar. Try the cupboard under the stairs, the spare room, the back of a wardrobe, an old freezer cabinet in the garage and, at a pinch, a corner of the living room or the kitchen. Place racks away from appliances which give off heat. This means the fridge and freezer as well as the cooker.

What makes a good wine?

There are numerous factors which affect the quality and flavour of the wine in the bottle.

Geographical location and climate are important. Vines grow between the latitudes of 50°N and 30°N in the northern hemisphere and in a similar band in the southern hemisphere. Beyond these limits the climate is either too hot to allow the vines a resting period in the winter or too cold to give enough sunshine to ripen the grapes properly.

Within these bands there are large variations in both climate and soil structure and these will substantially affect the nature of the finished wine. The climatic or weather factors also change from year to year to give vintage variations.

Other factors are rather more within our control. They include methods of viticulture, wine production techniques, and methods of aging. Some of these are fixed by tradition or by the appellation laws. Others are at the discretion of the grower and wine-maker.

Everything that happens to the vine - from pruning in late winter through flowering, fruiting and harvesting in summer and autumn to the crushing and fermenting of the grapes in the winery - will have a bearing on the flavour and quality of the finished wine.

Grapes which are harvested just as soon as they are ripe will give a different kind of wine to those which are left on the vine until they are affected with noble rot (see page 142) or are frozen into solid ice. Similarly juice which is fermented in vast steel tanks under controlled temperatures will taste quite different to juice which is fermented in open vats or in wooden casks.

With so many variable factors it is not surprisingly that wines taste so very different. However, you do not really need to know the detail of how all these factors affect the wine to know if a wine is good or not. It is good, it will taste good. But for those who are interested in learning a little more about the effect all these factors might have had on the bottle you picking off the shelves, read on.

The vineyard year

Before the grapes even reach the winery, a year's hard work has gone into the vineyard. In the northern hemisphere the year starts after the vintage in October or early November and in the southern hemisphere in February and March.

WINTER

The vineyards are generally tidied and ploughed now and the soil is built up round the roots to protect the vine if cold weather is expected. General maintenance is carried out. Earth may be carted from lower terraces to higher ones and manure will be dug in. In the late winter, the vines are pruned and the roots are cleared of soil.

SPRING

The shoots begin to grow now and they are fastened to wires or trellises in complicated patterns according to local custom. This is followed by the first spraying with pesticides. Vines are prone to various diseases and since prevention is better than trying to tackle a disease after it has started, spraying will continue through the summer until the harvest.

SUMMER

Flowering and pollination is followed by the setting of the fruit. There may be a summer pruning to stop the leaves taking over and to allow the grapes to get more sunshine.

AUTUMN

The grapes reach their maturity and sugar levels are measured. The grapes are gathered laboriously by hand, or rather more quickly by mechanical means. This usually means special machines which straddle the rows and gulp in the fruit. These monstrosities are both cost-effective and fast - an important factor if the weather is threatening rain. However, they cannot be selective and fine wine and wines with noble rot (see below) are still harvested by hand.

Growers will each have their own ideas on how, and exactly when, to conduct these many tasks in order to make good wine.

For example some growers hardly use any artificial fertilisers and keep pesticides to a minimum. Others spray with a variety of substances on as many as 14 occasions. The vineyards and surrounding areas can end up blue with spray.

There are moves to reduce sprays and organic farmers (see page 15) are trying to eliminate them altogether.

Noble rot

Much of the spraying that does go on is to protect against botrytis or rot. But there is one kind of rot which growers really welcome. This is a fungus which attacks the grapes, causing them to shrivel up. This is not as bad as it sounds, because the result is an intensification of the sugar content of the affected grapes and a kind of raisin-like quality which gives a very special taste to wines made from them.

Noble rot only occurs in certain weather conditions and so some years a vineyard may remain unaffected. This can be quite serious when you consider that the very best Sauternes, for example, are dependent upon noble rot for their quality.

It is an expensive business making wines from these grapes because each one has to be gathered by hand. Lesser wines may include the whole of an affected bunch, but the very best use only the affected grapes. Their juice takes quite a long time to ferment and the wines are usually better if they are kept for a year or two. Thus scarcity, labour intensity and storage all contribute to the high price.

The winery year

Some growers also own their own wineries and will thus be able to oversee the progress of their grapes into the finished wine. These people usually give some indication on the label (Château bottled etc. See page 155) that this has been the case. But more often the grapes are sent to large privately-owned or co-operative wineries where grapes from different vineyards are mixed.

For much of the year, the winery is a relatively quiet place with wine maturing in vats or casks and only routine racking and bottling going on. In the autumn the pace hots up and the place becomes a hive of activity. The grapes are delivered and their sugar levels are checked and the wine-making process begins.

The first step in wine-making is to crush the grapes to release the juice. This really did used to be done by foot. This is rare today, though I have seen men on stilts working the grapes for special port wines. Instead machines have been developed which will crush the grapes and, for white wine, separate the juice from the skins.

Red grape juice is fermented with the skins. This is because it is the skins which give most of the colour. Peel a red grape and you will see that the flesh is pale green in colour.

If you have ever wondered how they manage to make the almost colourless blush wines from Zinfandel and Cabernet Sauvignon - both red grape varieties - it is because the skins are removed before the wine is fermented.

Tannin also comes largely from the skins and pips and as this is not required in white wine, so grape juice for white wine is largely fermented without the skins. However, some producers are experimenting with leaving the skins of white grapes in contact with the juice for a short time to improve the flavours.

Fermentation

Fermentation will take place quite naturally as the yeasts, present on the fruit when they were picked, get to work. However, this can be a chancy business and most wine-makers add their own culture of yeasts. Sugar in the form of grape juice, acids and sulphur dioxide may also be added at this stage.

From now on the wine must be protected from the oxygen in the air. From very early times adding sulphur was found to be the simplest method of doing this. Some wine-makers are rather too enthusiastic with their use of sulphur and this can show up as a rather nasty smell coming out of the bottle as you open it. It is like the smell which lingers after you have struck a match.

Not everyone is sensitive to this smell, but sulphur is bad for people with asthma or who have breathing problems and some tasters will immediately start to cough if they encounter much sulphur. It is this additive which can also be blamed for some, though by no means all, of the hangover you may get from over-indulgence.

During fermentation the yeasts work on the fruit sugars and convert them to carbon dioxide. This is given off in the form of bubbles and alcohol when all the sugar has been used up or the alcoholic content reaches around 15 per cent by volume fermentation stops. This may take three days, three weeks or even three months. It depends largely on the temperature and with modern techniques the wine-maker can control the temperature in his vats.

Cold fermentation

The introduction of cold fermentation techniques using cooling and refrigeration plants has revolutionised the production of white wine in the hotter areas of Europe.

Instead of producing a variable wine, which in really hot years we would probably find undrinkable, huge plants have been built which their owners are fond of describing as 'Cathedrals of wine'. They have gleaming columns of stainless steel vats and have a kind of hum of clinical efficiency about them far removed from the romantic idea of wine-making. They have enabled the wine-makers of La Mancha in Spain, the Veneto in Italy or the lower Rhône valley in France to produce a clean, fresh wine every year.

The trouble was that some of them got so good at it that they also removed all the individuality from their wines. They all ended up tasting much the same.

There is a kind of boiled sweets smell and taste which is prevalent in cold fermentation wines made with cultured yeasts which can over-ride the character of the grapes themselves. This is as true of the usually characterful Chardonnay as the dull Trebbiano. Today many wine-makers have recognised the fault and are doing much to overcome the problem.

Sometimes fermentation is stopped before all the sugar has been used up and this results in a medium dry or a sweet wine. But not all sweet wines are made in this way. In some cases the sugar content is just too much for the yeast cells to tackle and they just give up.

As the wine ferments, small particles of dead yeast and other debris (lees) fall out of the solution to the bottom. The wine will be syphoned off the lees after a while to another container. But some wines are left on their lees until they are bottled (Muscadet Sur Lie for example).

The majority of white wines spend all their time in large concrete or stainless steel tanks. In the spring after the vintage, they are cleared or filtered and bottled. Some of the mass-produced wines are centrifuged or even heat-treated to ensure that there will not be a single speck of anything to mar the clarity of the wine. There probably won't be much flavour left either.

Incidentally, if you do encounter many coloured crystals in the bottom of your bottle of white wine, don't worry. Indeed, you should rejoice. It is quite harmless and proves that your wine has not been subjected to the rigours of modern technology.

Oak

A few white wines are put to mature for a while in oak casks and this gives them a distinctive oaky taste. White Rioja used to be made in this way and it had a great deal of character. Sadly, much of it is now made to taste like any other cold fermentation wine.

The Australians, New Zealanders and Californians are not afraid to experiment with oak and some of their Chardonnays, Semillons and Sauvignon or Fumé wines show the benefit. Wine growers in other areas such as Bordeaux and the Midi are also starting to use more oak in their white wines. Sometimes it works and sometimes it does not. The tendency is for the oak to smother the fruit.

Red wine is much more likely to spend some time in wooden barrels and oak is the timber most often used. Time in the barrel not only enhances the maturing process, but adds extra flavour to the wine.

The woody taste imparted by new oak has become so popular that some lesser wines seem to be overwhelmed by it. There is little else to taste. But when used with care oak can give a wonderful smoky quality which tasters often describe as 'vanilla'.

Finally the wine is bottled. Flavours marry up in the bottle and a fine wine may be left to mature for many years. But this costs money and unless you buy your own in the early years, you are unlikely to be able to buy many older wines in the high street.

It is easy to outline what appears to be the fairly simple process of wine-making. But in practice it is much more complicated. Decisions have to be taken at every stage and each decision will substantially affect the taste and style of the wine.

The methods which are used are many and varied. They can range from simple time-honoured techniques with little movement of the wine through more elaborate filtering and maturing processes, to high-tech systems, using sophisticated protein filters, centrifusion and automatic bottling plants.

With such a profusion of methods, it is not surprising that each wine turns out to be quite different from another and I am not just talking about one region from another, but from one winery to another and the second may be just down the road!

Champagne

Champagne is the sparkling wine. It spells triumph, special occasions and celebration. Drink it when you are in love, when you are successful or just simply for the joy of it.

Champagne really does stand at the top as one of the world's really great wines. It has quality and finesse. Its bubbles don't peter out after a few minutes, it has a distinctive flavour all its own and it lasts.

Even non-vintage Champagne improves in the bottle. Try keeping a bottle or two for six months or a year and it really improves. So, if you possibly can, try and buy well before that special occasion. Doing this also helps to spread the cost of the function over a longer period of time, but you must be strong-minded and keep your hands off the bottles!

Champagne is made by fermenting out white wine (often extracted from black grapes as well as white) and giving it another fermentation in its own sealed up bottle. This infuses the wine with bubbles.

The sediment which is created in this period of fermentation in the bottle is expelled by a neck-freezing and ejection process. The loss of liquid volume is then made up by adding a mixture of sugar and wine - the more sugar the sweeter the end result. A cork is inserted and the wine is left to mature for at least three years.

To many people it is enough to see the word Champagne

on the bottle, but as the price of this wonderful wine moves steadily higher, it is well worth making sure that you are getting value for money.

Not all Champagne tastes the same and like all wine the more expensive it is, the better it usually tastes. However, one or two of the supermarkets, such as **Waitrose**, **Morrisons** and **Sainsburys** have been able to come up with really first-class own-label Champagnes. Some of them also find small parcel of good wine which are put on sale at very reasonable prices at holiday times such as Christmas, so keep your eyes open.

Sparkling wines

There are plenty of sparkling wines other than Champagne and some of them can be very enjoyable indeed. There is something about drinking a wine with bubbles in it which lifts the spirits and transports the imagination.

All the countries which produce still wine also produce sparkling wine. France offers sparking Saumur and Bourgogne, Clairette de Die and Blanquette de Limoux, to name but a few. German sparklers are labelled Sekt and Spanish ones Cava. Italy sends us the sweetly perfumed Asti Spumante as well as some drier styles and California produces good but expensive sparklers.

The real challenge to traditional French sparkling wine has come from Australia and New Zealand and there are some very reasonably priced sparkling wines on offer from these two countries. If you have a little more to spend you might also consider wines like Deutz Marlborough Cuvée and Crozer which have been made in conjunction with some of the famous Champagne houses and which ironically are seriously challenging real Champagne in the UK market.

Sparkling wines made in the same way as Champagne have been labelled 'methode Champenoise', but the Champagne houses have objected to this and from August 1994 this term can no longer be used on labels. Phrases such as 'traditional method' or 'bottle fermented' will be used instead.

Other sparkling wines are made by fermenting the wine in the bottle to start with, then tanking, sweetening and filtering it back into bottles again. Some complete this whole fermentation and refermentation process in tanks. These wines will be labelled 'cuvée close', 'charmat' or 'tank fermented'. Others just have carbon dioxide forced into them. This is not really very successful as the bubbles do not last very long and the base wine is usually inferior.

The word 'brut', which appears on the labels of sparkling wine and which is supposed to designate dry wine, does not always mean quite the same degree of dryness. The description seems to have become almost obligatory and covers a multitude of sugar contents.

'Sec', which should also mean dry, often merely means medium dry, whereas 'demi-sec' and 'doux' are sweet.

Asti spumante

If you have a sweet tooth this is the wine for you and even if you haven't it is a wine which is well worth trying with dessert. It has become vastly underrated in the rush not to be considered unsophisticated.

The process by which Asti is made is an unusual one. The juice is extracted from the Muscat grapes, filtered and chilled to 0°C. It remains at this temperature until the wine is wanted in the market place. The required amount of juice is then warmed and partly fermented in an open tank, which is then sealed for the rest of the fermentation. The wine gains its bubbles during this latter period. Moscato Spumante is made in the same way, but from grapes grown outside the Asti district.

Because of the storage and fermentation technique, the wine retains a wonderful degree of freshness. So it is wise to buy newly acquired stock if you possibly can and to enjoy the wine very soon thereafter.

Fortified wines

These are wines which have been fortified with an extra dose of alcohol. Brandy is added to the wine at some stage in its production and the alcohol content shoots up from 10-15 per cent alcohol by volume to 18-22 per cent alcohol by volume.

Port, sherry, Masala and Madeira all come under the category of fortified wines, but they are all quite different in the grape varieties they use and in their methods of production. And of course, they all taste quite different.

Port

There's much more to port than the ruby port which goes into 'port and lemon' and the vintage port which is reverentially passed round at the regimental dinner.

But all ports start off with the fermentation of very sweet grape juice. The fermentation is stopped fairly early on by the addition of brandy - the yeasts just give up in the presence of so much alcohol and so the wine remains pretty sweet. Much of the fruity flavours are also retained.

The wine is then put into casks and left to mature. The impurities settle at the bottom of the barrel and the clear wine is drawn off from above (racked).

Ruby is kept in casks for about three to four years, racked, blended, filtered, bottled, shipped and drunk. It is a very young wine in port terms, but very drinkable for all that.

Tawny of 'every day' quality, may be a blend of white and ruby port. Or the bright red colour may have been removed from ruby port by a charcoal filter. Both techniques can produce this style. In fact, these tawnies may have spent less time in casks than rubies and are often inferior. This is the kind of tawny you will get if you order it on the Continent, where it is very popular.

True aged tawny is made like ruby, blended but kept in cask for much longer until it naturally pales in colour and gains a nutty taste. The best will have an age (average of the wines in its blend) of some ten to 40 years. This compiled number will usually be stated on the label. Connoisseurs may prefer the older wines, but ten year old tawnies are cheaper and exceedingly good value for money. Tawnies are ready to drink and do not need decanting. They make wonderful after-dinner drinks.

Colheita port is a tawny port from a stated vintage.

White port is simply made with white grapes. It may be sweet or dry. It is best chilled and served as an aperitif.

Vintage port is made from the very finest grapes from a great year. It is, once more, made like ruby but it is bottled much earlier, usually after 22 to 31 months in casks. Then it is time for it to rest, lying down, for five to 25 years or more, when it will have become something very special, but also very expensive. It needs to be decanted before serving.

This all seems fairly straightforward, but it is now that the problems start for there are also crusted and single quinta ports, late bottled ports and all kinds of blends marketed under grand names, such as 'Vintage Reserve' or 'Chairman's Reserve'.

Crusted port and *single quinta* ports can be treated as a simpler type of vintage. They may mature earlier than genuine vintage port, but will still need decanting. Single quinta port is made from the grapes of a single vineyard, usually in slightly lesser years than vintage ones. A word of caution here, for single quintas can also be tawny ports and Quinta da Noval is the name of a port house and does not make all its wine from a single vineyard.

Most of the blended ports are designed to be a substitute for vintage port and should, therefore, be cheaper. Some are excellent, others less so. *LBV* (late bottled vintage) is one of the most popular and fast growing styles of port and it is now made to be very approachable at a fairly young age. It is made with the grapes of a single harvest, treated with great care and retained in cask for longer than vintage and thus throwing off most, if not all, of its impurities before reaching the bottles.

Names such as 'Chairman's Choice' or 'Special Reserve' and indeed 'Vintage style', 'Reserve' or 'Character' are all actually elevated ruby ports. Most of them will improve a little in the bottle and might just possibly throw a bit of a sediment.

Incidentally, a useful tip for deciding whether or not the port in the bottle is one for keeping ('laying down') and then decanting, or the kind to open and enjoy at once, is to look beneath the capsule at the cork. If this is the stopper type, or has a screwtop open, drink, enjoy and re-stopper it. If, on the other hand, the cork is a *long* single piece driven cork, the wine is for keeping and should be treated as a vintage.

Sherry

Unlike port, this Spanish invention starts off as fully

fermented-out (dry) wine. It is then casked with a gap left between the wine level and the bung. On the surface of the liquid may grow a 'flor' (a layer of yeast). This wine is later fortified to make fine dry Finos, Manzanillas and then Amontillados.

Sometimes the wine does not develop flor and then the wine is fortified to make Oloroso wines. Some of these wines are also sweetened, particularly for export markets such as our own. In Spain most sherry is dry.

Manzanilla are Fino (dry) style wines, matured north-west of Jerez de la Frontera (the centre of sherry production) near the sea at Sanlucar de Barramida. They are dry and delicate - some say salty.

Finos are the finest dry white sherries - produced by the flor. To sweeten such wines is to ruin them though they are sweetened to make pale cream.

Some Fino wines are not considered good enough to bottle and are kept in the cask for longer. After a while the flor will degrade and the wine becomes a darker *Amontillado*. These are usually sweetened for the UK market.

Pale cortado is a very rare wine lying somewhere between an Amontillado and an *Oloroso*. It has the aroma of the former and the colour and taste of the latter. Its name literally means cut stick which refers to the chalk marks put on barrels of this wine.

Finally, there are the *Oloroso* wines (alias 'Milk', 'Cream', 'Brown' Amoroso and so on). These develop without the formation of flor and become oxidised because of it. In their natural state they are strongly flavoured and dry - although the glycerine in them gives them a feeling of sweetness in the mouth. They are nearly all sweetened for the export market.

The sweetening agent for good sherries is produced from the juice of Pedro Ximenez grapes that have been dried in the sun. This blending wine is produced separately from other sherries and it does not taste very nice on its own. However, it does wonders when mixed in to produce fine sweet sherries.

There is another unique process that makes fine sherry so good and ensures continuity in style and quality. This is the solera system - a method by which the wine in barrel that is ready to be bottled is partly bled off, to be topped up with younger wine from other casks. It is a complicated and finely judged process.

Top quality sherries tend to be expensive, but when you

consider the time and effort that go into their making they are very good value indeed. Cheaper sherries do not have quite the same depths of quality, but can still be very pleasant to drink.

At one time we drank far more sherry in the UK than we do now. No serious meal would have been without it as an aperitif or served with the soup. It still makes a good pre-eating drink, but I think I would probably put it in the soup (to pep up a good consommé for example). In Spain they are inclined to drink it throughout the meal; dry to start with and sweet with the dessert. The latter idea works very well with rich plum puddings or even chocolate gâteau.

Non-Spanish 'sherry'

Sherry is made in Spain - and nowhere else. But similar styles of fortified wine are made in South Africa, Cyprus and even Great Britain. They have been distinguished from the Spanish original by virtue of the fact that the label carried the word 'sherry' only in conjunction with the name of the country of origin, such as 'Cyprus sherry'.

The sherry producers of Jerez have been untiring in their efforts to get the word sherry removed from these copies and at long last they have succeeded. From December 1995 the word sherry will only be used on the labels of Spanish wines. The others will have to stick to the words fortified wine or dream up another name altogether. The copies are often much cheaper than the real thing and if you forget about the taste of or have never tasted Spanish sherry then they make pleasant drinks.

Vins doux naturels

These are lusciously sweet wines (mainly white) produced in the south of France. They differ from other dessert wines in that they do not acquire their sweetness from the natural sugar residing after fermentation. Rather, the fermentation is stopped fairly early on (like port) by the addition of brandy.

The term 'vins doux naturels' was coined in the nineteenth century as a tax avoidance scheme. When the French government announced a tax on fortified wines, the wine-makers of the south protested that they were already penalised by the low yields from their grapes. An exception was granted and the wines became known as 'vins doux naturels'.

The best known of these wines is Muscat de Beaumes de Venise from the Rhône valley. Trendy restaurants led a revival in dessert wines in the eighties and this was the wine which was pushed the most and, indeed, it is very good.

But, there are very similar (and cheaper) wines which come mainly from Roussillon in south-west France. They are Muscat de Rivesaltes, Banyuls and Maury. Producers of the first of these are keenly promoting their wines at the present time.

Wine scandals

Most wine-producing countries produce their wine according to set rules and regulations which cover grape varieties, yields, production methods and labelling. They are designed to maintain a basic level of quality, create and maintain specific styles in each area and prevent fraud.

However, it is a sad fact of life that wine is easy to 'doctor' and from time to time a grower or a wine-maker will get greedy and decide to take a few short cuts. Others have decided to 'enhance' their wine in a bad year by adding substances which subsequently turn out, at best, to be illegal or at worse poisonous.

Sometimes wine from one area is used to boost that from another area and labels have been known to be changed after a wine failed to sell. An identical wine may be offered under more than one own-label or presented under several different guises and prices.

But, don't get too despondent, these occurrences are rare. In the long run such practices simply do not pay and the wine trade is a fundamentally honest one. Producers are usually extremely proud of their product and only rarely accept that there is any need for improvement anyway.

Wine-growing regions of the world

Although wines from adjacent vineyards can vary tremendously in character, the major wine-producing regions of the world do have particular characteristics in their wines, which relate primarily to climate, soil type and the types of grapes used in the wines. In this outline of the major wine-growing regions of the world, we look at some of those characteristics and also give you some guidelines on understanding the various classifications of wine which are used in different countries.

France

French wines remain the most popular of wines. Nearly 40 per cent of all the wine drunk in the UK is French. The wines are divided into four categories: Vin de Table, Vin de Pays, VDQS (Vin Délimites de Qualité Supérieure) and AC (Appellation Contrôlée). These categories give an indication of origin and (though not a guarantee) of quality.

Encompassing sparkling, red, rosé and white wines, *Vin de Table* is the humblest French quality level and denotes an anonymous wine or blend of wines which may come from anywhere in France. They take in anything from rough local wines to multi-blend brands, such as Piat d'Or.

Vin de Pays is a superior Vin de Table category which was introduced in the seventies to try and encourage growers to use superior grape varieties and better wine-making methods. The wines sport attractive names such as the Loire's Vin de Pays du Jardin de la France and Corsica's Vin de Pays de L'Isle de Beauté.

The ploy has been so successful that some of the best bargains in the high street carry this denomination.

A notch up from Vin de Pays is *VDQS*, but the category is rapidly diminishing as growers opt for quality not quantity and are upgraded to full *AC*.

The French AC laws are designed to preserve what the French wine authority considers to be typical of a region. You, on the other hand, may prefer the a-typical grape varieties used by a Vin de Pays producer down the road.

The level of quality of a wine will always appear on the label, but it may be in very small type. Indeed, the most important phrases tend to be tucked away under much grander-sounding words. Look out for significant phrases such as 'mis en bouteille au château' or 'au domaine'. This means that the wine has been bottled by the property which produced it and is usually a sure sign of quality.

Compare this to the rather similar 'mis en bouteille par Monsieur X, a negociant at Y', which means that the wine was bottled by merchant X in the French town in which he happens to be based. Of course, if you have often bought Monsieur X's wine and found it to your taste, this information is equally useful.

Phrases which are merely there to hype the wine include 'grand vin', 'selection speciale', 'cuvée speciale', 'extra reserve'. Ignore them for they are all meaningless. The label must also include details of the quantity contained in the bottle and may also give the percentage level of alcohol by volume.

Bordeaux

Claret is the name we English have given to wines from this area of south-west France. The châteaux which produce the top wines are among the most famous wine names in the world. They include Lafitte, Latour, Mouton Rothschild and Petrus. These wines are superlatively good and priced to match and they never reach the high street shelves. They are to be found only in the cellars of the rich, or in the international sales room.

But lower down the scale come wines from the minor châteaux that, in a good year, can reach their own superlative heights. These are the ones to remember and seek out. So, vintages can be important here (see page 12). If a run of good vintages occurs then the high quality will even find its way down to basic or generic 'Claret', 'Bordeaux', 'Médoc' or 'Bordeaux Supérieur' wines. Just such a run of good vintages occurred in 1988, 1989 and 1990.

Unfortunately the run came to an end with extreme frosts in the spring of 1991. The 1992 vintage looks better with standards possibly reaching those of 1988 but the wine will be ready to drink fairly early. Côtes de Bourg is reported to be a good bet among the cheaper reds. Reports on the 1993 vintage are also quite good, but it is early days yet.

Claret has a very special taste and style of its own. It is made from a blend of Cabernet Sauvignon, Cabernet Franc and Merlot grapes and it tends to have less fruity flavours and more woody (though not oaky) flavours than some other wines. When this has mellowed with a little age the results can be tremendous.

But a great deal of wine is produced in Bordeaux and much of it is sold without much ageing at all and it can be both tannic and acidic. However, thanks perhaps to growing competition from other areas of France and, indeed, other parts of the world, a much more fruity and easy-to-drink style is emerging among the cheaper wines.

There are dry white wines from Bordeaux too, especially from Entre-Deux-Mer and Graves. Sauvignon-based wines are becoming increasingly successful and rightly so, for they have good character and flavour without being over fresh or sharp. It is not usually possible to tell from the label how much of the this grape variety has been used in the mix. Some supermarkets have asked their suppliers to give this useful information on the label but the French wine authorities are not in favour and may ban the practice.

And finally, don't forget the sweet wines of Bordeaux. Some of the best sweet wines in the world are made here in Sauternes and Barsac. Again, prices can be high, but look out for St Croix-du-Mont and Loupiac which are cheaper and can be very good too.

Burgundy (from Chablis to Beaujolais)

Burgundy vies with Bordeaux for the role of 'top wine-maker'. Some enthusiasts prefer one; some the other. I will come clean and confess that when I can afford it, I side with the Burgundy lovers. The problem is that supply is limited and the best are very expensive, the lesser costly enough.

The problem is compounded by the fact that buying Burgundy can be fraught with disappointment. Some of the most famous vineyards are divided between 30, 40 or even 50 different owners and Gevrey-Chambertin from one grower may be quite sublime, whereas that from another more slapdash producer may be quite dreadful. The only way through the minefield is to remember the names on the small print. Except for Beaujolais and a wine called Passtoutgrain, the red wine is made exclusively from the Pinot Noir grape.

Burgundy is a long drawn out area and the styles of wine vary. It would be a mistake to think of it as a single entity. It takes in Chablis in the north and runs south along the river Soane to Beaujolais country, just north of Lyons.

Chablis might be one of the best known white wines in the world, but when it is outside the control of the EU, it may not have anything to do with Chablis at all. If you encounter 'Chablis' in Australia (things are now changing here) or California, it could be any old dry white wine and it is rarely made from Chardonnay, the grape variety which must be used in the denominated region of France.

Mind you, the amount of genuine Chablis drunk everywhere seems to be much greater than the region could possibly produce. This may be because many Petit Chablis have been up-graded to Chablis and many ordinary Chablis to Premier Cru. This has enabled a good deal of extra planting to take place. There is a suggestion that Petit Chablis should be phased out altogether. If this happens it will be a disaster for it will be even more difficult to predict the quality of the wine in the bottle.

To my mind, most Chablis is already overpriced, but if you do encounter a good one, buy it and keep for a while. It will reward your patience.

Move south to Dijon and the Côte d'Or and you move into what most people think of as Burgundy. The Côte d'Or (golden hillside) is made up of the Côte de Nuits in the north and the Côte de Beaune in the south. Awe-inspiring names include Nuits-St- Georges, Clos de Vougeot, Gevrey-Chambertin, Corton and Pommard among the red wines and Corton Charlemagne, Meursault and Montrachet among the white.

Names to look out for are the Hautes-Côtes de Nuits and the Hautes-Côtes de Beaune - what they lack in finesse, they make up for in value, but they will still take you over the £5.00 mark. 1991 was a better vintage here than in Bordeaux. 1992 is likely to be variable with the top growths offering better value than the Hautes-Côtes and Villages. 1993 is looking hopeful.

Chardonnay is the grape used for classic whites in Burgundy, but wine is also made from the Aligote grape. This is relatively cheaper and in good years can offer good value for money.

Moving south again past the improving Mâcon (red and white) and the overpriced Pouilly Fuissé, we come to the Beaujolais. This used to be a good hunting ground for easy-to-drink wines. Made from the Gamay grape they did not cost an arm and a leg. Some of them lasted well too. Sadly the price of Beaujolais has now risen to the point where one begins to wonder if it is really worth it. After all you can find some very drinkable wines in a similar style from the Loire.

Beaujolais wine is it quite different to that of the rest of Burgundy. Most of it is made by a process called carbonic maceration. The wine is fermented under pressure with the skins. This extracts as much of the fruity flavour as possible and results in a bright purple coloured wine with bags of taste.

A large, though now declining, percentage of all production is turned into Nouveau. This wine is rushed through to be ready for sale in late November. Its quality is often a good indication of the success or otherwise of the forthcoming vintage from the region.

Folklore has it that Nouveau should be drunk before Christmas. In fact, in a good year, Nouveau will last well into the following year. In France it is often on sale throughout the following summer. In a bad year it's probably better not drunk at all!

The better wine from the region is called Beaujolais Village or carries the name of one of the ten 'special' Beaujolais villages of Saint Armour, Julienas, Chenas, Moulin à Vent, Fleurie Chiroubles, Morgon, Brouilly, Côte de Brouilly and Regnie. These wines can last for four or five years and Moulin à Vent can go on for ten or more years when it will have taken on some of the flavours of its more exalted fellows to the north.

The Loire

With one or two exceptions, the wines of the Loire are light, refreshing, happy-go-lucky wines. They are as good to drink on their own as they are with food. You will not get great complexity of flavour, but you will be able to have a lot of fruit at a reasonable price.

Muscadet must be by far the best known wine of the Loire. It comes from a region whose capacity to produce wine seems mysteriously to increase every year. Nantes is the centre of production and some of the more expensive Muscadets are sold in special bottles which have a shape exclusive to the area.

Muscadet is dry and, at its best, reasonably fruity. It is often recommended as a wine to serve with fish, particularly shellfish. Sèvre-et-Maine, often to be seen on labels, is the major producing area.

Another term sometimes seen on the label is 'sur lie'. This means that the fermenting wine has been allowed to continue sitting on its yeast and fruit residues (lees) until it is bottled. The wine has a more intense flavour and often has a slightly spritzy or fizzy taste on the tongue. It is well worth the extra money you will have to pay for it.

Nearer to the Atlantic is grown a grape variety called Gros Plant. This is particularly astringent on the palate and is something of an acquired taste, though the locals reckon it partners fish even better than Muscadet.

As you continue up river to Anjou, the grape varieties change. Light white wines are made from both the Chenin Blanc and Sauvignon grapes and, of course, the popular Anjou Rosé comes from here, too. This well-known wine is getting drier as our tastes move that way and it is good for easy drinking throughout the year. A good dry rosé is Rosé de Loire.

Also from the Anjou district come the much underrated sweet Coteaux du Layon wines and a very pleasant light red - Anjou Rouge. As well as being a good buy, the latter wine will give you an idea of how the Loire reds taste.

This leads us upstream to the Saumur region where light, still wines, both red and white, are made, as well as some delicious sparking wines. They are uncomplicated and appealing. From here too comes the red Saumur Champigny, a pleasant light red wine.

Upstream again to Bourgueil and Chinon. These are the red stars of the river. They are made from the Cabernet Franc grape and will age for up to five years, but they can also be very attractive in their youth. A lesser known red is Touraine Gamay which has a touch of light Beaujolais tastes in its make-up. More light and easy-to-drink whites here too, mainly known by their regional name of 'Touraine'.

Vouvray is one of the best known white wines from this part of the river and this is usually on the sweeter side, the finest making excellent dessert wines. Vouvray comes in dry and sparkling versions too. Montlouis is another name to look out for from this area.

Much further up-river is Pouilly-Sur-Loire where the very classy and expensive Pouilly Fumé is made and to Sancerre which can be almost as pricey. Sauvignon Blanc is the grape variety here and it is certainly seen at its best. Quincy is a name to watch for. This area produces wines which are similar in style to Sancerre but which are usually rather cheaper.

Alsace

For some reason Alsace wine is often known as the wine merchant's wine. Perhaps because it is not so well known to the general public. It might also be known as the wine-writers' wine as it is certainly among my favourites.

In recent years supermarkets have offered wines from Alsace under their own label. Some of these are good, but it has to be said that the more you pay for wines from this area, the better flavoured they are likely to be.

Unlike the wines from other classic area of France, Alsace wines are classified (and marked on the labels) by grape variety rather than by properties or vineyards. All the wines have a particularly fruity flavour, more reminiscent of German wines than French, but they are completely dry - a fact often disputed by friends who try them for the first time.

Perhaps the best one to start with is either the Riesling or the Pinot Blanc. The step from German to Alsace Riesling will not result in too unfamiliar a flavour or, if you are a Chardonnay fan, you may be very pleased by the taste of Pinot Blanc.

Much more striking and, therefore, much more of an acquired taste are Tokay Pinot Gris and Gewürztraminer. A sip of one of these wines can be a real mouthful it is so intense (full of citrus fruits and lychees - Australian wine lovers should enjoy them). However, styles vary and some are really flowery, others more spicy in nature. So try a few to find one to suit your palate and then buy a few bottles to keep. Muscat d'Alsace offers the flavour of Muscat grapes (usually sweet) in a dry style.

Merchants will tell you that Alsace wines should be drunk young and, indeed, they are very good then, but you can reap some real taste rewards by keeping them for two or even three and four years.

Edelzwicker is the local table wine. It is a blend of grape varieties and is just the thing to knock back with your choucroute or jamboneau if you should visit the region. Some shops do also stock it in the UK.

In recent years new legislation has defined a number of specific vineyards which are allowed to identify themselves as DOC Alsace Grand Crus. Only four grape varieties can be used (Riesling, Gewürztraminer, Tokay Pinot Gris and Muscat d'Alsace) and maximum yields are strictly controlled. These wines are expensive and do not nearly come within my £5.00 limit. Sadly this is now the case with almost all Alsace wines.

The Rhône

The Upper Rhône produces grand, deeply-coloured and robust wines from the Syrah grape. If you don't mind a fair bit of tannin, they can be drunk young with strongly flavoured food, such as game and winter stews. However, the more expensive ones are made to keep. The high street offers some of the lesser wines, such as Crozes Hermitage and St-Joseph, but they are mostly beyond our £5.00 limit.

The lower Rhône is the home of Côtes-du-Rhône wines, as well as Châteauneuf-du-Pape, Gigondas and Vacqueras. Sadly, Côtes-du-Rhône wines present something of a minefield. They can offer excellent value for money, or they can be very bad.

Some of the wines are quite peppery with plenty of taste and character, others are medium-bodied and quite fruity and yet others are thin and rather nasty and the only way to sort out one from another is to try them. Price may be a help here, but it won't help you sort out the best of the fruity wines made by carbonic maceration and the older tougher style wines.

In addition to the valley of the Rhône itself the area also takes in regions such as Vaucluse, Luberon (Mayle country), Tricastin and Ventoux which are situated in the hills of northern Provence. Most of the wines here are light and easy drinking with plenty of fruit.

Further south in the Bouche du Rhône, the light and summery Listel Gris is produced from grapes grown on the sands of the Rhône delta. Provence is also a great rosé wine-producing area. More and more of these prettily coloured and increasingly flavourful wines are finding their way to the UK as wine-producing standards rise.

French country wines

In general terms, French country wines have come to mean all those wines that come from outside the classic regions. These wines continue to go from strength to strength in the supermarkets and high street chains with wines coming from as far afield as Bergerac in the Dordogne valley just outside the Bordeaux Appellation to Fitou on the Mediterranean coast and the Côte de Provence in the south-east. They are not nearly so expensive as their classic cousins.

Bergerac produces wines which are very reminiscent of Bordeaux, which is not surprising when you look at the proximity of the two areas and the fact that they use the same grape varieties (Cabernet Franc, Merlot and Cabernet Sauvignon for red wines and Semillon and Sauvignon Blanc for white wines). White Bergerac can be very pleasant but it is the red wines which are particularly good. They usually have plenty of fruit as well as a good structure (worth keeping for a year or so in good years).

Fitou forms part of the crescent of wine-producing areas which skirt the Mediterranean from Perpignon in the west to Toulon and Nice in the east. The wines here are usually pretty full-bodied with good depth and colour. The wines of neighbouring Rousillon (1993 was an exceptional year here), Coteaux de Languedoc (also very good in 1993) and Corbières are usually (but not always) rather lighter. The best are full of bramble fruit flavours.

As quality improves growers are keen to emphasise the regional quality of their wines and to distinguish their own areas from others. Corbières, for one, plans to sub-divide into 11 crus (villages), so stand by to remember even more names from this up and coming part of the wine world.

Cahors, Minervois, Madiran, St Chinian, Gaillac and Jurançon are some of the other appellations of south-west France which can be found on the supermarket shelves. The best are full and fruity but some of them can be very tannic. Cahors and Madiran, for example, use the local red Tannat grape and this can give a very thick and rustic wines which is something of an acquired taste. So much so, in fact, that Cahors was often known as the 'black wine'.

Today young growers are making even more tannic wines by ageing Tannat in oak! The co-operatives, on the other hand, with an eye to foreign tastes, favour a lighter, more approachable style of wine and add Cabernet Franc or Cabernet Sauvignon. You will probably have to take pot luck to find out which is which.

Growers in all the non-classic areas are grading up both their grape varieties and their wines. Thanks to heavy competition from Australia and more recently from Eastern Europe and South America they have had to get their act together and start using modern techniques on a much wider scale. The result is a range of first class red wines, made from both local and classic grape varieties, which are designed to be drunk two or sometimes three years after the vintage.

These wines may not yet be great names to boast about but, even with the current unfavourable exchange rates, are good value for money. The whites do not usually reach quite such a high standard but some growers are experimenting very successfully with local grapes such as Terret as well as the ubiquitous Chardonnay and Sauvignon Blanc.

Should you have a taste for sweet dessert wines, try Montbazillac and Jurançon Moelleux (just sweet) with their almondy flavours. These wines from the south-west compare well with the more expensive dessert wines from Sauternes and Barsac.

Vin de Pays wines

On some wine lists the phrase 'French country wines' mean Vin de Pays wines. These wines first appeared on our high street shelves about five years ago. Now they dominate the cheaper end of the French market. There are Vin de Pays areas in all the wine growing regions of France and supermarket wine buyers seem to vie with each other in exploring in new areas. Names such as Vins de Pays des Côtes de Gascogne, de l'Aude, d'Oc, de l'Hérault and de St Mont are now commonplace.

Names which were new to the UK last year include Vins de Pays de Mont Caume, Vin de Pays des Coteaux du Quercy and Vin de Pays de l'Ardaillhou. This year brings Vin de Pays des Coteaux de Cabrerisse and Vin de Pays des Côtes de Perignan.

Many of these Vin de Pays areas simply offer a blend of local grape varieties but increasingly they are offering varietal (single grape variety) wines such as Chardonnay, Merlot and Cabernet Sauvignon. Vin de Pays d'Oc, particularly, has led the way with most producers offering varietal wines. Others worth looking out for are Vin de Pays du Jardin de la France Chardonnay and Gamay and Vin de Pays de l'Hérault, Terret and Syrah.

Vin de Pays wines are made to be drunk the year after the vintage but the odd Cabernet Sauvignon may respond to a year in the cellar. Just don't keep it for too long.

Germany

Germany is the great white wine-producing country of Europe. It lies at the climatic limit for growing vines and red varieties, though they exist, do not flourish in great quantity. German wine imports account for 27 per cent of UK wines sales. As much of this is still Liebfraumilch, I have again given this blend a section to itself (see page 168).

Traditionally German wines have been sweet. This is because the grapes tend to produce very acidic wines which would not be very palatable on their own. Thus the practice of adding unfermented grape juice (süsswein) to the lesser wines has grown up and this results in medium dry to medium sweet wines.

Having said this, the fashionable trend in Germany has been to produce dry (trocken) or slightly less dry (halbtrocken) wines which do not have the added sweetness. The idea is that they will be better suited to being drunk with food. Some of these wines have been exceedingly acidic and so harsh that they are not at all attractive. However, things are improving and it is not only the more expensive quality levels which produce good wine in this style.

The Germans have revised their wine laws on numerous occasions but, generally speaking, they grade their wine on the ripeness or sweetness levels of the grape juice and this is clearly stated on the labels. This means that except at the lowest levels, the riper the grapes, the better the wine will be. The key words to look out for are:

Tafelwein means table wine. This is a blend of wines from EU countries, rarely German, which is bottled in Germany.

Deutscher Tafelwein is a German blend of table wine.

Landwein is special table wine coming from a stated area equivalent to the French Vin de Pays category.

Qualitätswein bestimmer Anbaugebiete (QbA or Quality Wine) is an every day wine from a particular region. Most German wines fall into this category. They come from specific regions and often sound a lot grander than they are.

Qualitätswein mit Predikat (QmP) is wine with special distinction and these distinctions are, in ascending order:

Kabinett, Spätlese, Auslese, Beerenauslese, Eiswein and Trockenbeerenauslese.

Kabinett is light and usually drier than the rest (though sweeter than a Spätlese trocken or halbtrocken). They are superior to QbA wines because the sweetness comes from the natural sugar in the grape juice, not from the addition of süsswein. They may also be produced in trocken and halbtrocken form.

Spätlese (late harvest) has more flavour. They may also be produced in trocken and halbtrocken form and these are often the best of the German dry wines.

Auslese is wine made from selected and very ripe bunches which produce sweet wine.

Beerenauslese wines are made from selectively picked grapes and are rare, rich and sweet dessert wines. They are usually very expensive.

Eiswein is a sweet wine made from grapes gathered frozen from the vines. Again, it is very expensive.

Trochenbeerenauslese is a very sweet wine made from almost raisin-dry grapes. It is highly concentrated in every way.

Tafelwein to QmP Kabinett wines are best drunk the year after the vintage, though Kabinett wines can be kept in a good year. The rest mature beautifully with age. Indeed Beerenauslese, Eiswein and Trockenbeerenauslese need at least a year or two and preferably five to ten to reach their full potential.

Sichel Riesling Kabinett

1988 Wachenheimer Bischofsgarten

Rheinpfalz

Qualitätswein mit Prädikat Produce of Germany

Estate Bottled by Winzergenossenschaft Wachtenburg-Luginsland, Wachenheim

Shipped by

75 cl H. Sichel Sons Ltd., London WC2N 6JP

e A. P. Nr. 514 23 73 140/89 10.0 % vol

German labels all carry an AP or official test number which tells (from left to right) where the wine was examined, where produced, the producer's code number, the number of the particular lot or bottling and the year.

German wine regions

The most frequently seen wine regions in the UK are Mosel, Rheingau (one of the best), Rheinhessen, Rheinpfalz and Baden. The name of the district printed on the wine label can help to give you some idea of the wine inside, but only some idea because each estate may produce many styles of wine each year and these can vary from bone dry through to very sweet.

In addition, 27 different grape varieties may be used and those used in one year's vintage may differ from another. So, making a reasonable guess at what lies within a bottle of German wine is not an easy business. The best wines are made from the Riesling grape but there are other varieties such as Müller-Thurgau, Kerner, Schreuebe and Weissburgunden producing different styles.

Mosel wines are usually quite light and delicate. They have a crispness which balances their sweetness. Piesporter from the Bernkastel area is a particularly well-known name, though like some other popular names there is rather more of it about than there seems room for vineyards.

Slightly to the north-east the Rheingau produces the classic wines of Germany. It was with wines from this area that Queen Victoria is said to have coined the word 'hock'. Made from the great Riesling grape they are elegant and fruity with plenty of acidity to balance the sweetness. They can cost much more than we normally think of paying for a German wine, but they are excellent.

Wines from the Nahe can relate to those of Mosel to the west or to Rheinhessen in the east and are rather variable. My father's favourite wine came from this region and so I have rather a soft spot for the good ones which are usually very fruity.

Franken wines are offered in flagon-shaped bottles, rather like the Mateus Rosé bottle. In fact the latter were adapted from the Franconian original! They are distinguished by their fuller more gutsy flavours. They are often dryer than other German wines. They are also rather more expensive and quite difficult to find in the UK.

Rheinhessen is the original home-ground of Liebfraumilch (see later). The wine from the area is generally light and flowery and easy to drink. One of the best known names from the region is Niersteiner.

Moving south to the Rheinplatz - a big producer - and Baden the wine gets rather flatter and fuller, though there are exceptions. The better wines come from the northern parts of the region.

German wines are often looked down upon by aspiring wine-drinkers who believe the propaganda that bone dry is best. This is just not true. There have been a lot of bland and sugary wines coming out of Germany, but there are also some really delicious wines which are perfect to serve as a winter aperitif or to drink on a summer's picnic.

How to find these wines is, I admit, more difficult. Some supermarkets have attempted to solve the problem by simply labelling their wines Kabinett, Spätlese etc. or using the regional name in large letters. Fuller details are given in small type.

Here is a simple guide which I hope will help you to be more adventurous when choosing wines labelled in the German style:

1. Ignore the long names which you cannot pronounce.
2. Look at the region from which the wine comes.
3. Pick the quality and sweetness level you want - Kabinett or Spätlese trocken are probably the best to start with.
4. If possible check the grape varieties - this can be difficult as in many cases it is simply not given.

Leibfraumilch

Liebfraumilch is important because so much of it is drunk. It regularly tops the list of supermarket best-sellers. So for those of you who have not heard the story, here it is again. (Other readers can skip to the next section.)

When the Romans reached Worms, in Germany, they found that the wine made there was delicious and more delicate than the existing litre daily ration wine to which their legionnaires were entitled. So they fostered the wine industry to reduce the burden on their lines of supply.

The Dark Ages came and went and wine continued to be made in that same area. In medieval times, monks built a church there and called it the Liebfrauenkirch (Church of Our Lady). They, too, tended the vines.

In the eighteenth century, an Englishman called Maximillion Mission, returned home from Worms and wrote a book. He referred to the wine as being so delicious that the monks thought it to be as sweet as milk from the Holy Virgin. And that was the first record of the name Liebfrau(en)milch used as a description of this wine.

Since then, however, the name has been bastardised to the extent that at one time most of the wine from Germany was referred to as Liebfraumilch - and some of what came from Austria and Alsace too.

Rules have now tightened up and Liebfraumilch must now be a quality German wine of purely German origin. The main grape varieties are Riesling, Silvaner, Müller-Thurgau and Kerner and current legislation states that the blend must contain at least 70 per cent of these classical varieties. This increases the level from the previous 50 per cent. The remaining 3 per cent may be made up of up to seven or more different grape varieties.

Surprisingly, although this white wine is our nation's favourite, the Germans hardly touch a drop of it. This probably because they do not have any difficulty in pronouncing the long German names!

The price of Liebfraumilch varies enormously and so does the quality and flavour. Some of the cheaper ones are good value for money but some are very boring indeed. So shop around and buy two or three different ones to see which you like the best.

The brand leaders such as Blue Nun are not more expensive just because they spend so very much more on marketing and advertising (though this is of course a factor). They do also care very deeply about the quality of their product and even some Kabinett wines find their way into the Blue Nun blend. However, with the new laws the difference may not be as great as it used to be.

Nearly every wine shop in the high street sells this most popular of wines, so I have not bothered to list it in the shopping sections.

Italy

Vines grow along the length and breadth of Italy. The grapes they produce are made into every conceivable style and quality of wine. Many of them are very reasonably priced and high street wine buyers are beginning to introduce an exciting range of unfamiliar wines at affordable prices. Nearly all of them will be good wines to serve with food, so take the plunge and try one next time you buy a wine to serve with the meal.

In the past it has sometimes been difficult to tell exactly what to expect from the contents of a bottle of Italian wine before opening it. However that is all set to change, for at long last the Italian system of classification is to be overhauled. New wine laws were passed early in 1992 and, though there are bound to be modifications caused by problems with implementation, it does look as if major reforms are going through.

The strange anomaly of *Vino da Tavola* (or table wine) which is more expensive than top class DOCG wine will, hopefully, disappear. So too should the situation where a first class single estate Chianti from the Classico zone has exactly the same status as a mass-produced wine from an inferior area. However the full extent of the changes will probably not be felt in the UK high street for some time to come.

The new law provides for the establishment of a pyramid system of classification which includes both a geographical and a quality element.

At the base of the pyramid are the Vino da Tavola wines. These are equivalent to the French Vin de Table wines.

IGT or Indicazione Geographiche Tipiche wines come next. This is a brand new category roughly equivalent to French Vin de Pays or German Landwein. As well as the name of the area the label on these wines may also state the grape varieties.

It is expected that many current Vino da Tavola wines will be replaced by IGT wines but this will take some time to come about as the law stipulates that three years must pass before a Vino da Tavola can become an IGT wine. Eventually there will be around 150 IGT wines.

DOC (Deonominatione di Origine Controllata) wines form the next layer of the pyramid. At present there are 250 but a good 50 or more may disappear through lack of use. The place name or the name of the vineyard may be used on the labels of these wines.

DOCG is the highest of the Italian wine designations. There are currently thirteen of them: Albana di Romagna, Asti & Moscato Asti, Barbaresco, Barolo, Brunello di Montalcino, Carmignano, Chianti, Gattinara, Montefalco Sagrantino, Taurasi, Torgiano, Vernaccia di San Gimignano and the Vino Nobile di Montepulciano.

The new laws allow for small areas or microzones producing high quality wines to have their own DOC or DOCG classification. This applies even if the area coincides entirely with the property of a single owner. Thus a single estate Chianti, for example, could have its own designation.

In some ways the new regulations should have the best elements of both French and German wine law. Wines can rise to the top of the pyramid or fall to the bottom depending upon the selection made at the harvest. The new law gives greater creative freedom to the wine-maker in that he can decide at the moment of the harvest - not a year earlier as has been the case - the type of denomination he should use.

That decision is now tied, as in Germany, to the quality of the grapes in a given season. For example, in the Montalcino area the producer will be able to decide whether to make a DOCG Brunello di Montalcino, a DOC Rosso di Montalcino or, in a particularly difficult year, an IGT or a simple Vino da Tavola. If the grower exceeds maximum yields the wine will automatically descend the quality pyramid.

Turning to label descriptions, the use of the word '*Superiore*' has been banned. However '*Classico*' denoting a wine that has come from the traditional heart of a region of production such as Chianti Classico, remains. So far does '*Riserva*' meaning a wine which has been specially selected and which has been aged for at least two years. The law also allows for the description '*Novello*' for wines similar to the French Nouveau wines.

When these regulations have been fully implemented we should all have a much better idea of both the quality of the Italian wine we are buying and the area, commune, estate or vineyard from which it comes. In the meantime we shall have to battle on, checking price levels and endeavouring to remember the name of the best wine-makers in each region!

It is probably worth mentioning here that Italian wines

were traditionally made to drink with food. They usually have a high acidity and dry finish which partners the rich pasta sauces, game sausages and roast meats of the local cuisine. The Italian is not used to the idea that you might want a wine to smell and taste fruity, or that you may want to drink wine on its own. So a slice of salami, some stuffed olives or a cube of Pecorino cheese will still enhance your enjoyment of many of them.

Of course, things are changing and so-called flying wine-makers like New Zealander Kym Milne and Aussie Geoff Merrill have begun to work with local producers to make modern wines have much more fruity flavours.

Tuscany and Piedmont

These are the homelands of Italy's most famous red wines. Piedmont produces Barolo and its slightly lighter cousin Barbaresco. Even at their best, these are tough and tannic wines and I have not found many within my price limit that I would be prepared to drink. At their worst, they are dried out and harsh. However, things look set to change in this area as growers start to experiment with aging in new oak barrel and with other modern techniques.

Piedmont is also the home of Asti Spumante (see page 148) and the other famous Moscato wines. A light red wine from this area which is fun to drink is Barbera d'Asti. It can be highly acidic but it does have lots of fruit and flavour. Nearby are the white wines of Gavi. These are pleasant enough but have suffered from a good deal of hype in recent years and they tend to cost a lot more than they should.

The word Tuscany is synonymous with Chianti. This famous red wine can reach the heights, but sadly it can also plunge the depths and, unless you know the names of all the growers and vineyards, it can be a bit of a minefield. Wines from Classico and Ruffino regions are probably the best bet, but trial and error is the only way to find the ones you like.

Good Chianti does not really come under our £5.00 umbrella and those that do are often just trading on the name. The best of these wines are made to last, so if you do decide to splash out give them a year or two before starting to drink them. 1992 and the new 1993 are both worth buying to keep.

Some people bemoan the passing of the traditional round straw-covered bottles or fiaschi and make the mistake of rushing out to buy a bottle or two if they see them abroad. Unless you want to make a lamp, don't do it. The Tuscans derisively pack their lesser wines in these bottles to sell at vast cost to the Japanese and the Americans!

From the south of the region come three fine reds in Vino Nobile di Montipulciano, Brunello di Montalcino and the rather cheaper and excellent value for money Rosso di Montalcino.

There are just a couple of whites worth trying here. They are the flinty-tasting Vernaccia di San Gimignano and Galestro, but, sadly, as they grow in popularity, so their price ascends.

North-west Italy

This large wine-producing area stretches from the Trentino/Alto Adige at the northern end of lake Garda through the Veneto to Lombardy and Emiglia Romana. It offers a huge diversity of indigenous varieties which the adventurous shopper should revel in. There are also excellent wines made from more familiar varieties such as Merlot, Cabernet Sauvignon and Chardonnay.

The Trentino/Alto Adige (South Tyrol or Sud Tirol) is a mountainous district in the north where a number of French and German grape varieties, such as Chardonnay, Pinot Blanc and Gewürztraminer, are grown with some success. A light red to look for here is Lago di Caldaro. It is almost more rosé than red and has a mountain freshness to it. Another favourite of mine is Teroldego Rotaliano drunk young - up to two or three years.

The Veneto region, inland from Venice, is famous for Soave, Valpolicella and Bardolino. These are well-known wines which, in the past, had been mass-produced into a boring uniformity. However, things are beginning to change, and Valpolicella, in particular, offers a deliciously fruity drink. Some of the Classico versions are very good indeed.

Another big producer is Friuli-Venezia Guilia. The best wines are full of fresh fruity flavours and the area grows traditional grape varieties as well as experimenting very successfully with French varieties, such as Merlot and Tocai (Pinot Gris). Lombardy merits a mention for its Lugana white wine made from the usually much more boring Trebbiano grape.

Much further south you will arrive at Emilia Romagna, Lambrusco capital of the world. This wine follows Liebfraumilch in being one of the biggest supermarket sellers. If you like its sweetish semi-sparkling style, it is probably worth spending just a little more for the DOC editions, such as Lambrusco di Sorbara, Reggiano, Grasparossa di Castelvetro and Salamino di Santa Croce.

Central and southern Italy

The best known wines from central Italy are white. They include Verdicchio from the Marches, Orvieto from Umbria and Frascati from Latium.

The problems of making wine in a hot country have here, as elsewhere, been solved by the introduction of cold fermentation techniques. The result is clean, well made wines which all taste very much alike. It is particularly important to look for the word 'classico' on the label. These are usually the better wines and some of them may have been made by growers who have reverted to more traditional methods and have thus regained their individual flavours.

Don't be seduced by the romantic name of Campania's best known wine La Cryma Christi or 'Tears of Christ' for the story is much better than the wine. It is said that when Christ looked down from heaven on the Gulf of Naples he was so moved by its beauty that he wept.

A red wine from central Italy which is usually very good value for money is Montepulciano d'Abruzzo. This is made from a local grape variety in the hills over looking the Adriatic coast. It is no relation to Vino Nobile di Montepulciano.

Sardinia is producing good wines at reasonable prices and further south Sicily is beginning to turn out some lovely jammy wine which are full of warm ripe fruit and very attractive. Look out, too, for the excellent Terre di Ginestra wines among the more expensive wines. They are labelled Vino da Tavola, but are as good as many DOC wines. Good value, too, are the Salentino wines from the heel of Italy.

Spain

Spain's DO (Denominacion de Origen) system is virtually in line with the French AC system but in 1991 a new quality status was introduced - the DOC (Denomination de Origen Calificada). It has been granted only to Rioja and seems to reflect the improvement in the system of wine controls that the region has put into place over the last ten years and the respect that Rioja commands in the market place.

The very best Spanish wines need some time to age and luckily for us the wine-makers do most of the ageing for us. No need to buy in young and store under the stairs. Aim for the *Crianza* (with ageing) quality. If you like okay tasting wines, this applies to white as well as red wines. Crianza means that the wine has spent some time in old oak casks and a further time in the bottle before being sold.

Below this quality you may possibly still see CVC printed on the back label (meaning mixed vintages) or, more likely now, Sin Crianza meaning without oak aging. Above Crianza quality come *Reserva* and *Gran Reserva*. These wines have more and yet more oak and bottle age - the actual amounts depending where it comes from and whether it is a white or a red wine.

Thanks to modern technology, Spain is also increasingly offering young fresh wines from non-classic areas which are ready to drink.

Rioja

Rioja was the great Spanish success story. The introduction of this wine to our high street shops changed the image of Spanish wine for ever. No longer just 'plonk', Spanish wine had quality. The original Riojas, both red and white, were hefty, oaky wines, the best still with plenty of fruit.

The whites were the first to bow to the wind of change. The public demanded fresh, easy-to-drink white wines and traditional Rioja was characterful and demanding. Only a few of these, such as the wonderful Marqués de Murrieta, remain, the rest are cold fermentation look-alikes which could almost have come from southern France or Italy.

Sadly, it looks as though the reds may go the same way. Apparently, the world demands easy-drinking fruity reds as well and the Spaniards are determined not to lose out. To my mind though they will lose out and, even more, if the traditional character of a great red Rioja is lost to general mediocrity. Some growers are fighting for their traditional wines. A new Gran Reserva Club has been set up in the UK to sell and promote this style of wine. Members will be offered newly released wines are they come onto the market.

Even more controversial are the questions of how much Cabernet Sauvignon should be added to the traditional Tempranillo and whether or not the wine should be matured in American or French oak. Mention Cabernet Sauvignon to the Spanish traditionalist and he rapidly becomes very heated indeed. However, while some producers do use quite appreciable amounts of this popular grape variety others are experimenting with indigenous varieties like Garnacha. Hopefully the result will be a wider range of interesting wines.

Vintages to look for include 1985, 1987 and 1989. Heavy rain badly affected the 1988 harvest and the same thing has happened in 1992 and 1993.

Penedès and the rest

This has been another success story. Here wine-makers had no classic wine to sell. They have experimented from the start and, led by the New World, the famous Torres Company have produced a variety of first-class reds and whites made both from traditional Spanish grape varieties and from French varieties or blends of the two.

Penedès is also the home of Cava (Spain's sparkling wines). These are made by the Champagne method - indeed, wine-makers here reckon it was their forebears who taught the Champagnoise, not the other way round! The wines are crisp and dry with a slightly earthy flavour. The best are very good value for money. Some of these, too, are beginning to see the benefits of some French grapes!

Navarra wines have had something of a chequered career. Sometimes, like lighter, fruitier Rioja and sometimes over-acidic and boring, they seem to be improving now. Other areas to look out for are Ribera del Duero, Rueda and Lerida.

Bargains are now to be found among wines from Valdepeñas. This area is offering attractively mature wines with plenty of fruit. La Mancha and Jumilla are other areas which are beginning to make use of modern technology and there is now less need to tread with care. The many examples brought in by the supermarket wine buyers are usually very easy drinking well made wines.

Portugal

Portuguese wines taste different and that for me is their attraction. Some are made to improve with age and these tend to arrive in Britain when they are almost ready to drink. Compared with the classic wines of France or Italy they are on sale at bargain prices. Other wines are made to drink a good deal earlier than was previously the case and many of them are very attractive.

The last five years have seen a quiet revolution in wine-making in Portugal. Port has always had a wide international reputation - though it is rather surprisingly less popular on the home market - but table wines have not been noted for their excellence. A few isolated reds have been good enough to find their way to the UK but most Portuguese wines were best left for sale at the local roadside tasca or wine taverna.

All this has now changed. Increased demand on the domestic market coupled with Portugal's entry into the EU have led to unprecedented investment in vineyards and wineries. As brand new stainless steel vats and refrigeration plants are going into place tired and oxidised white wines are transformed into clean fresh wines with good fruit and stewed reds, dried out over long periods in cement vats, are now emerging full of wonderful ripe fruit flavours.

Portugal's *Regiao Demarcada* or DO system is similar to that elsewhere, but it has only recently started to expand the number of its designated areas. Evora is one new area and there are other in the pipeline. Look out for the word *Reserva* on a Portuguese label, it usually indicates a wine of excellent quality. *Garrafeira* indicates 0.5 per cent more alcohol and a specially selected wine aged in cask for two years plus one in bottle. *Velho* often used with the word *Tinto* (red) means old or traditional.

Portugal is one of the few countries which has resisted the temptation to plant popular French grape varieties such as Chardonnay and Cabernet Sauvignon. Perhaps this is because it has some 80 or more different varieties of its own.

In the past vineyards were often planted with a number of different grape varieties mixed in together but modern growers are beginning to weed out the inferior varieties and concentrate on those which research has shown to produce the best results. Names include Touriga National (also used in port), Baga, Castelao France or 'Periquita'.

Most people would probably be hard put to name any of Portugal's wine regions but Dão might just spring to mind. This used to be mooted as the classic red wine of Portugal after port but to my mind most of them were far too tannic and dried out to be enjoyable. The red wines of Bairrada can have the same faults. However, efforts are being made to improve the wines from these areas. Tannin limitation is the name of the game and it is beginning to work. Look out for the name Quinta dos Carvalhais from Dão and Caves Alianca from Bairrada. White Barriada made from Roupeiro grapes can be a good buy.

At the present time the Douro, Ribentejo and Alentejo offer better value for money. The Alentejo, in particular, often makes wines which are softer and easier to drink. Tannins are not a problem here. Borba (one of the five sub-regions) is offering wonderfully fresh reds packed with cherry flavours and Portalegre (another sub-region) has an excellent smoky oak-aged red, and also Tinto da Anfora (JP Vinhos).

Vinho Verde is the other Portuguese wine style which is pretty well known. The first of these white wines arrived 20 years ago and they established themselves as a cheap, heavily sweetened alternative to Liebfraumilch. Today most of them are still on the sweet side but there are a growing number of single quinta (estate) wines making very fresh crisp wines from grapes grown on the estate. Don't expect the usual sweetness in these wines; they are, to quote one expert in the field, whistle-dry.

Eastern Europe

The wines of Eastern Europe, sometimes more poetically known as the wines of the Danube, have caused a real stir in the high street over the last year or so. They offer a good alternative to French Vin de Pays wines and cheap wines from central Spain or southern Italy.

Bulgarian wine came on the scene some time ago but the lifting of the Iron Curtain has allowed more wines from Hungary, the Czech Republic, Slovakia, Romania and the newly formed Moldova to find their way here too.

Of course, the whole area is in a state of economic and political turmoil (what was Yugoslavia is already the victim of gross upheaval and only a few wines from this area get to the shops here.) and there is no certainty about how the wine business will go. But a number of entrepreneurial wine-makers like Hugh Ryman, wine buyers like Angela Muir and the Australian production team from Penfolds have seen the potential and have leaped in with both feet. Big business, too, is beginning to take an interest and money as well as expertise is moving eastwards.

The results so far have been very good. Whether the prices will remain as competitive as they have been is very unlikely, so buy while you can. Indeed some prices have already started to climb.

Austria

Austrian wine is making a slow come back onto the supermarket and high street shelves after some years in the doldrums. The new Austrian wine laws are extremely stringent. These together with the self-assessment which took place in the wine industry after the so-called wine scandal of the early eighties have led to the re-emergence of a range of drinkable, well-made wines.

The classification system for Austrian wines operates in a similar manner to the German laws in that they are based not on location but on the sugar content of the grape juice and most wines helpfully state the grape variety. However, Austrian wines should not be thought of as just another type of German wine. They tend to be drier and to have a definite style of their own.

A large percentage of Austrian wine is based on the local Grüner Veltliner grape variety. This grape produces dry and medium dry wines with a distinctive fruity or spicy character. It is fresh and zingy in its first year but can mellow to a more honeyed flavour after a year or two.

Wine producers are also making excellent wines from other varieties such as Pinot Blanc, Pinot Gris and Gewürztraminer. At their best these are beginning to rival those of Alsace. Chardonnay and Weissburgunder are also on the list. Light and easy drinking red wines, too, are also beginning to appear on the market and these are based on Pinot Noir or the local Zweigelt. They have little tannin but lots of fruit.

In the past, it was always the sweet wines of Austria which commanded the highest praises and this is still true today. Look out for Beerenauslese and Trockenbeerenauslese wines. They are full of dried fruit and caramel flavours which are as good if not better than their German counterparts and they are still somewhat cheaper.

Environmentally conscious readers may like to know that one leading producer - the Lenz Moser Company - is replacing all lead, aluminium and plastic wine bottle capsules (the covering around the neck area) with paper seals. They estimate that they will make annual savings of around 10 tons of environmentally unfriendly material. Who will be the first to follow suit, I wonder?

Bulgaria

Bulgarian wine sales boomed in the UK market in the eighties, soaring from 95,000 cases in 1982 to nearly 2 million in 1990. Bulgarian Cabernet Sauvignon regularly appears in the list of top ten supermarket best-sellers. Despite the recession and the price increases resulting from three budgets, sales remain steady.

In the last few years the Bulgarian wine industry has faced a series of crises. First of all, hard-line communists ploughed up a third or more of the Bulgarian vineyards in a misguided attempt to follow Mikhail Gorbachev's anti-alcohol campaign in Russia in the mid-eighties. This has resulted in a decreasing quantity of wine for export to growing markets.

Secondly the post communist upheavals resulted in 1990 in the new government giving the wineries a few hours (quite literally) to set up as independent trading companies. The monopoly on export agencies is gradually being eroded and Bulgarian Vintners, once the only UK importer, now faces competition both in buying the wine as well as in selling it in the UK. The first private Bulgarian company to be set up was Domaine Boyar which represents the wineries of Burgos, Stara Dagora, Preslav and Suhindol. Other private companies are currently in the making. This should mean keen competition and therefore keen prices in the high street.

The third major change came with the introduction of the Land Reform Act. This allows for the restoration of land to its pre-1945 owners (this should have been completed by January 1993). This could be good news for wineries (who to date have owned few vineyards) in that they might be able to buy from owners who are not interested in viticulture. But it could also mean the some producers will find their vineyards divided up into small individually owned parcels.

So far all this has resulted in price increases not decreases. The days of the £1.99 bottle of Bulgarian wine are well and truly over but there are still good buys to be had at the around the £3.00-3.50 mark. Bulgarian wineries are fighting the growing popularity of French Vin de Pays wines in this price range by producing their own Country Wines.

These Country Wines are mainly blends of grape varieties

181

They usually include local varieties with one of those two most popular of grape varieties - Chardonnay and Cabernet Sauvignon. Excellent examples are Cabernet/Cinsault from Russe, Chardonnay/Misket from Sungurlare, Riesling/Dimiat from Khan Krum, Merlot/Pinot Noir from Sliven and the highly successful Merlot/Gamza from Suhindol.

Cabernet Sauvignon remains the star buy for Bulgarian wine but it is a mistake to think that there is only one type. Each winery is developing its own style of wine and it is well worth while starting to remember winery names - luckily most of them are easier to pronounce than German or Hungarian estate names.

Suhindol was the first Cabernet Sauvignon to hit the British market, but there are now at least eight. Look out for Russe, Sakar Mountain, Oriachoritza, Melnik and Pavlikeni. Pulden (Plovdiv) also makes a good Cabernet and an excellent Cabernet/Mavrud. Stambulovo and Sakar produce first-class Merlot. Khan Krum was well known for its Chardonnay but today Chardonnay from Varna and Sliven is better. Also very good is rosé from Burgas.

Red wines made from local varieties such as Gamza and Mavrud have been less popular; but when it is well made, Gamza has an attractive fruity flavour which falls somewhere between a Beaujolais and a Burgundian Pinot Noir. Mavrud tends to be much heavier, but it can mature well.

Bulgarian quality levels are fairly easy to follow. First of all there are the *Country Wines*. These use blends of grapes to produce a fruity flavoured, easy drinking wine. In fact some are better than their more expensive brothers and sisters.

Next come the *Varietal Wines*. These are made from single grape varieties from specified regions. They usually have more backbone and tannin than Country Wines, though they are still designed to be drunk while they are young.

Reserve Wines must be aged in oak casks for a least two years for white wines and three years for red wines. If the wine is well made and full of fruit to start with this treatment will only enhance them. If not, the results can be tired and bitter. Because of the time factor, you will have to pay more for these wines.

The most expensive, and in theory the best wines, are the *Controliren Wines*. The vineyards producing grapes for these wines are exactly defined by area and are chosen and designated for specific grape varieties. The same problems that beset Reserve Wines also apply here. There are some very good Controliren Wines but you will need to go cautiously and try each variety and vintage before buying more than one bottle.

Vintages which have been universally good are 1988, 1990 and 1991. For red wine, 1990 is said to be the best vintage since 1954 but the cooler damper weather in 1991 produced good white wines with a higher acidity which may be preferable in the 1990s. 1992 was reasonable for both red and white.

The Czech Republic and Slovakia

This area has one of the longest established wine industries in Europe. It has a climate similar to Austria and Alsace but it is also warm enough to ripen Cabernet Sauvignon grapes. In theory, it should be able to produce wines to rival those of Bulgaria, and maybe even to challenge some classic areas of the West.

The problem is that the doctrinaire policies of the Communist regime led to disease in the vineyards, over-production and bad wine. Considerable investment will be needed to put things right and this could be a chancy business.

First of all ownership of the vineyards has to be established - original owners can apply for restitution, traditional markets in the East have dried up and there is unlikely to be a government subsidy to keep prices down. In addition wine making equipment is outdated and standards of hygiene are difficult to maintain.

Despite this depressing picture some reasonable wine is being made, both from French varieties such as Pinot Blanc and Cabernet Sauvignon and from local grape varieties such as Irsay Oliver and Frankovka. The former is a spicy and grapey white and the latter a ripe and juicy light red wine.

These wines were the result of a superb effort by Angela Muir MW who almost single-handedly bullied the wine-makers of Slovakia into taking more care with their wine-making. She has been followed by Nick Butler and there will be others.

Hungary

Hungary has a long tradition of wine-making, but most of it was consumed at home or went to Russia. A small amount did find its way to the UK via a single export agency. The picture then changed radically. There is no longer a monopoly on agencies and the bottom has fallen out of the Russian market. Despite the abundance of grapes and labour, most Hungarian wineries have not had the expertise to produce wine of sufficient quality to sell in the sophisticated markets of the West.

But the possibilities are there and in 1991 some young wine-makers from the West took advantage of the new detente with the East and took their wine making skills to a part of the world where the climate had not interfered with the vintage.

Gyongyos Estate was at the forefront of this new development. Here Hugh Ryman and Australian wine-maker Adrian Wing are producing good clean Chardonnay, Muscat and Sauvignon wines in sufficient quantities to supply quite a number of high street outlets.

Other producers have flocked to follow in their footsteps. Italian wine-maker Pietro Antinori is working with a new company called the European Wine Producers in the Szekszard region, Jerry Lockspeiser of the Leeds-based company Bottle Green has got together with another Australian, Nick Butler, and Master of Wine Kym Milne has been working at Balaton-Boglar. There is no doubt that Hungary is now set to produce wine to rival the success of Bulgarian wine.

Indeed, most of the Hungarian wines in the high street now offer good value for money. Regional names to look out for inlcude Nagyrede, Villany and Szekszard. Useful brand names are Volcanic Hills, Lake Balaton, Dunavar and Chapel Hills.

The best known Hungarian wine in the UK used to be Bull's Blood. The story goes that it was this wine which fortified the inhabitants of Eger in their battle against the invading Turks. When the Turks saw the Hungarians with their beards stained red from the wine, they turned and ran in terror, thinking that their enemies were drinking the blood of bulls!

So far most of the new wave wine-makers have played safe with well-known favourites such as Chardonnay and Cabernet

Sauvignon and the local grape varieties have largely been ignored. This may be because they are very difficult to pronounce. However, a few, like Kekfrankos, are beginning to find a place in the new order and more are expected to follow. So if you like to extend you knowledge of new or unfamiliar grape varieties watch this space.

Tokay (or Tokaji)

This wonderful sweet wine from Hungary is so special it deserves a section to itself. Historical tradition has it that it was first developed back in 1650 by a local monk or priest. He called his wine 'aszu' (sweet) and he made it by allowing the grapes to dry on the vine - producing a very concentrated paste.

Today the wine is made by picking individual grapes which are pressed and fermented. Then, according to the style desired, tubs (puttonyos) of aszu paste (the concentrate) are added to the brew. The number of these added tubs per barrel may be three, four, five or (rarely) six (Essencia). The wine is matured for two years longer than the number of puttonyos added.

So the more puttonyos the sweeter and older (and more expensive) will be the wine. The longer it is kept in bottle after this, the better it will be. On a visit to Hungary I tasted a 31-year old bottle of the five puttonyos, which tasted as good as the best Sauterne I have ever had.

Until 1991 all Tokaji wine-making was controlled by a Wine Trust. Since then the best estates have gradually been sold off to a number of different, largely Western, wine companies. Sadly the shake-up in ownership may mean a different approach to this wine. At a recent tasting the wines seemed to have lost some of their intensity.

Although not permitted to introduce new grape varieties or tamper with Hungary's complex appellation system, some of the new owners are making changes to the wines, moving away from the highly oxidised style of Tokaji Aszu to wines which have less bottle age and are fresher and fruitier. But are they Tokaji?

However, it is early days yet and other estates and owners may prefer to retain the old style. In the meantime try to buy the 1970 or early 1980 vintages if you can find them.

Moldovia

The independent republic of Moldova was declared on 27th August 1991. The country, which borders Romania in the west and the Ukraine in the east, used to form part of the former Soviet Union.

Wine-making has been established here since the mid-nineteenth century when European settlers were encouraged by the Russian rulers of the country to plant just those grape varieties which are so popular today, namely Chardonnay, Riesling, Cabernet Sauvignon and Merlot.

After the second world war the vineyards were nationalised and since then the industry has been hit by much the same problems as those which have beset the rest of eastern Europe. Today wine-makers are having to return to forgotten principles of clean wine-making and learn innovative techniques.

Hugh Ryman was, once again, one of the first to see the wine-producing potential of the region. He has persuaded the Penfolds, the leading Australian producers to get involved and their wines are being well received in the high street here. Flying wine-maker Jacques Lurton, with Dutch backing, is also about to venture into Moldova and there may be more Westerners on the way. Keep watching is the message from this promising area.

Romania

In the past, Romanian wine tended to be rather on the sweet side - red as well as white. This was the way that many people liked their wine and it was certainly the way the Russians liked it and Russia was Romania's main export market.

But, like the rest of Eastern Europe, there are signs that

things are changing. Romania is beginning to try and emulate Bulgaria in trading with the West. The most promising wine-making regions are to be found on the Carpathian foothills of Moldavia and towards the Black Sea coast where the climate is more temperate.

Despite the fact that Romania produces more wine even than Bulgaria so far only a small amount of Romanian wine finds its way to the UK. Romania's most exciting native grape is the white Tamaioasa. In its own country it is sometimes called the Frankincense grape and it makes a stunning vintage dessert wine. It is full of dried fruit flavours and caramel.

Good red wines from Romania can be difficult to find in the high street but the Prakova Region can produce good Cabernet Sauvignon and there are some really first class vegetal Pinot Noir wines around. Romania certainly has a good deal of catching up to do but along with the rest of eastern Europe it promises well for the future.

The Republics of former Yugoslavia

The wine industry in the former Yugoslavia, like most other industries in this currently war-torn country, has taken a bashing this year and it is uncertain whether much wine will be produced let alone shipped to the UK. However, some wine is getting through from Croatia and Macedonia.

Lutomer Laski Rizling was the Yugoslavian wine which most people knew, though small amounts of Gewürztraminer and Pinot Noir were beginning to appear on supermarket shelves last year.

The Laski Rizling should not be confused with the German, French or Austrian Riesling. It is quite a different grape variety and while it produces a fairly pleasant wine when it is well made, it does not compare to the classic variety.

Around the eastern Mediterranean

Few wines reach us from Islamic Turkey - though perfectly good wines seem to be on sale to holiday-makers in the country. Maybe they do not taste so good when you carry them back home.

Another holiday destination whose wines have not translated very well to the UK is Greece. However, things are beginning to change. Heavy investment in modern technology and the employment of highly qualified oenologists is beginning to result in much better wines. The trend started, with mixed results, in the small 'boutique' wineries often set up by shipping magnets as a kind of off-beat hobby.

More recently, larger outfits such as Tsantali, now the largest wine export in Greece, have also started to produce much cleaner, more attractive wines such as their white Peza, light red Makedonikos and heavier red Nemea. Other names to look out for include Château Semeli and Château Carras.

These wines are still not very well distributed, but you may come across them in specialist merchants. If you like Retsina (wine flavoured with pine resin during fermentation) the Tsantali version is particularly clean and fresh.

You may also find some of these wines in your local Greek restaurant - that is if it is really Greek. Most Greek restaurants are run by Greek Cypriots and it will be Cypriot wines that are on offer. The best that can be said of these is that they are straightforward, sunny wines which are not too demanding.

Château Musar, from the Lebanon, is a source of fine wine -though fairly expensive. Also fairly expensive are the Israeli wines, which are finding their way to the UK. Some of them (Yarden, for example) are very good, but cost more than our £5.00 limit.

All these wines have to compete for space with many more profitable, fast-selling (established) wines and so they would have to be particularly good value for money to get much more space than they have already.

English wine

English wine as distinct from British wine (see below) is no longer an irrelevant blip on the wine-making scene. A respectable three million bottles were produced from the 1991 harvest and three and a half million in 1992. There are now approximately 400 vineyards supplying 140 wineries and the industry is still expanding.

During the eighties, English wine was something of a joke to the general public. Not many people had tasted it; partly because it was not generally available and partly because it was expensive in relation to other wine. Most vineyards only produced enough to sell through their own shops and those that did sell to wholesalers were unable to supply the quantities required by the supermarkets.

In addition excise duty has to be paid on English wines at the same rate as foreign competitors (not the case in other European wine-producing countries). This, together with the small production levels, kept the price at an uncompetitively high level and until recently prices rarely fell below £4.50-5.00.

The bumper harvests of 1991 and 1992 changed all that. Excise duty remained the same but prices fell and some supermarkets were selling English wine for less than £3.50 a bottle. In addition to the one or two wines stocked by all outlets, supermarkets are also stocking a range of local wines in and around the areas in which they are produced. There is now no excuse not to support one of our newest and most successful industries.

So what does English wine taste like? First of all it is mainly white, either dry or off-dry. The commonest style is flowery and fragrant with a crisp acidity which us usually balanced by good fruit. They might be compared to a good German trocken or halbtrocken or sometimes to Alsace wines.

Other growers are producing distinctive styles based on hybrid grapes (crosses between American and European varieties) such as Seyval Blanc. Yet others are experimenting (very successfully) with sparkling wines and with red wines. In addition to Seyval Blanc, grape varieties include Müller-Thurgau (less popular then it used to be), Reichensteiner, Bacchus,

Kerner and Madeleine Angevine. Growers are trying out single varietal wines (try these to build up a taste memory of English grape flavours) and with different blends.

Under the EU Wine Regulations, English wine ranked only as table wine even though some can match the high quality of fine wines as proven by their performance in international competition. However, as production increased and we exceeded the 25,000 hectolitre mark a Quality Wine Scheme had to be put into place. The Pilot Scheme proposed by the Ministry of Agriculture in 1992 was not greeted with much pleasure by the growers.

Both the wine growing regions defined in it and the grape varieties allowed caused a good deal of controversy. Compromises have now been made on both sides and a new Quality Scheme defining English and Welsh wines has been agreed with the Ministry. Wines are divided into *English Table Wines* and *Welsh Table Wines* as the bottom tier with *English Vineyard Quality* wines and *Welsh Vineyard Quality* wines above them.

The other problem on grape varieties allowed has yet to be solved. Under English growing conditions hybrid grape varieties such as Seyval do much better than the accepted classics. EU wine law forbids the use of these vines in quality wines (though confusingly they are allowed in sparkling wine). The growers have suggested that there should be an intermediate class of Regional wine between Table and Vineyard Quality wines which would allow the use of hybrids. So far this has not been agreed with the EU.

Very few producers have taken up the opportunity to sell their wines as 'Quality'. This is partly because of the costs involved in dealing with the complicated application procedure and partly because many of the best wines use hybrid grapes.

Under the EU rules the crossing of the 25,000 hectolitre mark also meant that a ban should have been imposed on new plantings for anything other than quality wine. However, the weather in 1991 and 1992 was unusually clement and growers believe that they are unlikely to produce such large amounts every year. For once the Ministry has stood up for its own farmers and refused to apply the EU ban. Instead the English harvest will be monitored for five years and an average of production taken over that period. This at least gives growers a breathing space in which to increase plantings if they so wish.

British wine

It is with reluctance that I include British wines, but they are very popular. British wine is called British because it is processed, but not grown, here. Concentrated grape juice is imported and then made into wine, or 'sherry'. The processing which the juice undergoes is more extreme than in even the most highly technological winery and something is lost in the process.

Brand names include Rougemont Castle, Concorde, Country Carafe and Chambard. They are relatively cheap in price and, of course, this alone makes them attractive, but do remember that a few pence more per bottle and you could be drinking something much fresher and more attractive.

South Africa

South African wines are making something of a comeback in the high street. As political change continues in South Africa so sales resistance falls. There some good buys around but the South African wine industry is suffering from its years of isolation. Many growers and producers have been out of touch with world tastes.

However, current investment in equipment is high and change is in the air. Wine buyers in the UK are coming up with the goods and the choice is increasing all the time. So if you want to try South African wine you will need to know a little about the South African certification system. Wine-producers may choose to have their wines 'certified' and most who export do so.

The various classifications are indicated on the neck label in the form of coloured stripes. One Blue band (origin) means that 100 per cent of the wine in the bottle comes from the named district on the label. One Red band (vintage) indicates that at least 75 per cent of the wine inside is from the harvest year stated. The Green band (grape variety) means that prescribed minimum of the grape variety indicated is included and that the wine has the style of that variety.

The 'full house' of the above Blue, Red and Green bands combines their separate meanings with the guarantee that the wine is made from grapes grown on one specific estate, but that it may have been bottled elsewhere. Blue, Red and Green on a Gold background combines all the above and, in addition, shows that the wine had been assessed as a high quality South African wine.

South African wines may be sold as varietals or as blends. The grapes include Pinotage (a cross between Pinot Noir and Shiraz), Cabernet Sauvignon and vast quantities of Chenin Blanc (known as Steen) made into a huge range of styles. Increasingly there is also Chardonnay, Sauvignon Blanc and Colombard.

KWV (co-operative wine-growers association) is still the most widely distributed of the South African wines and they are quite good value for money (look for the brand name Cape Country at around £3.49). They also produce own-label wines for groups such as Marks and Spencer and these are very good indeed.

South Africa's top wines from wineries like Rustenberg, Klein Constantia and Boschendal tend to cost upwards of £7.00-8.00 and they are in danger of missing out in the £4.00-6.00 area. There still need to be more wines between the two price extremes and these are gradually starting to appear.

Australia

Australian wines were the sensation of the 1980s but they were not for the faint-hearted. They were powerfully flavoured, almost dense wines. These are still around but there are also some more restrained, even delicate wines on offer. Oak no longer dominates everything in sight. Australian wine-makers have settled down into producing their own styles of wine.

Australian wines put their emphasis on the grape variety (varietal) used rather than on where the wine is made and in the past there has been considerable movement of wine from one area to another. A wine labelled Cabernet Sauvignon from Barossa Valley, for example, can have up to 20 per cent wine from other varieties and districts blended into it.

At present there is no AC system, though some areas (Mudgee in New South Wales) do enforce their own appellation stamp through blind tasting and this could become more wide-spread. Under a new agreement with the EU, the Australians have agreed to divide their territory into new approved appellations. While this is being worked out they will limit the use of regional names such as Coonawarra to wines coming from those regions.

As Australian wine-makers define their own styles so we, the buyer, need to get to know which producers produce what style of wine. So take note of the name on the label when you find a wine which suits your palate.

Prices were expected to rise in the nineties but increases did not materialise. Indeed some prices went down. Quite a few supermarkets and off-licence chains introduced own-label wines from Australia or negotiated deals with specific growers and this helped to keep a good choice of Australian wines in the £3.50-4.50 price range. However, the Australian dollar is now extremely strong and it may not be long before the expected increase in prices really does happen.

Among the white wines, Chardonnay is the prima donna. Sometimes aged in oak, sometimes not, its full tropical flavours leap out of the glass at you, but do give a thought, too, to some of the other varietals.

Rhine Riesling (not so popular and, therefore not so

expensive) can be excellent. Forget any thoughts about German wine the word Riesling may give you. These are quite different and when they are oak-aged, they can be very good indeed.

So too can the Semillon and Chenin varietals and blends. The blends list their varietals in descending order of importance, so that a bottle labelled Semillon/Chenin will contain more Semillon than Chenin. Give them a try. Sauvignon, too, is in there, but the flavour difference between the Aussie and European versions is quite pronounced.

Among the red wines, Cabernet is king, but don't forget the Australian Shiraz (said to be similar to the Rhône Syrah) and the two together really make a winner. Some very good Pinot Noir is also beginning to emerge from Australia.

Cabernet Sauvignon is grown all over Australia, even at Alice Springs! Visitors have been known to travel by camel to Château Hornsby in central Australia. The vintage here traditionally starts on 1st January.

The sparkling wines of Australia are now of very good quality and good value too - some of the more straightforward costing as little as £5.00. At the other end of the scale Australia is producing some first class sparkling wines which are even beginning to rival those of Champagne.

New Zealand

The maritime climate of New Zealand seems to have favoured the production of white wine, though great strides are now being made in the production of red wine. Maybe it was just that the Yugoslavs, who first started growing vines, were more used to white varieties.

New Zealand wines are sometimes more delicate than Aussie wines, but they are still very well flavoured indeed. Their quality is first class, indeed some of the Chardonnays and Sauvignons equal, if not surpass, the quality of wine made from these grapes in France. But, once again, they are not cheap. You are unlikely to find a bottle much under £4.50 and the best will set you back from £6.00-£10.00.

Cooks and Timara wines are among those you are most likely to come across in the supermarket and they are both very good. Try the Chardonnay, of course, but also Gewürztraminer and the very light and pleasant Dry Reds. Montana is another great name. Their Sauvignon is world-famous and they also produce a good Rhine Riesling.

New Zealand wines have definitely 'arrived', but this means that they are in demand and prices may rise. So, if your spending limit is £5.00, grab a bottle or two now while you still can.

Sparkling wine from New Zealand is a new development. Deutz, the Champagne house, is working with Montana wines to produce a first class sparkling wine, which like those of Australia and California, rivals genuine Champagne.

The USA

There is so much wine now being produced in other areas of America (Washington States, Oregon) that American wine is no longer synonymous with California. However, few of these fall within our £5.00 limit and they are rarely seen in the high street.

California

California was the launching pad for American wine and Californian wine-makers have been very successful. Some producers have stuck to fine wines but others like Paul Masson and Gallo have developed huge wine 'factories' which produce very large quantities of wine indeed.

In the States, simple quaffing wines are sold under spurious names like 'Chablis' or 'Burgundy'. They haven't seen a Chardonnay grape, but they are pleasant, easy-drinking wines for all that. Under EU law this kind of labelling is not allowed and this level of wine is usually sold simply as California Dry (or Medium Dry) White or Red.

Like most New World wines, California's better wines are sold as varietals, but it is worth mentioning that if a grape varietal name is mentioned, only 75 per cent of the wine has to come from that variety. As elsewhere in the world, Cabernet Sauvignon and Chardonnay are the stars and the best ones are very good indeed, but they have been very expensive and so have not often appeared on the high street shelf.

However, wine consumption in the USA has fallen and harvests have continued to grow. As a result Californian wine producers have had to cast around for markets new and the UK looked to be a tempting prospect. Over the last year or so there has been an influx of wines in the £4.50-6.00 price range and a few supermarket own-label wines at an even lower price. This looks like good news. After all until recently there was very little good Californian wine under £8.00-10.00.

But the problem is that with one or two exceptions (such as Fetzer Fumé Blanc and Glen Ellen Proprietors Reserve Chardonnay) the whites are light and pleasant, but do not have very much character and who wants to pay £5.00 for a very ordinary wine when you can buy a first class Vin de Pays de Côtes de Gascogne for less than £4.00?

The pink or 'blush' wines are even worse value for money. These are usually made from surplus red grapes (Zinfandel and Cabernet) and sweetened with Muscat. They are sold as 'blush' as the producers are unable to eradicate the colour from the skins. Thankfully these wines seem to be on the decline in Britain.

Some red wines, particularly those made from Zinfandel and Pinot Noir, represent good value but taste before you buy in any quantity. On the whole those companies like Glen Ellen and Fetzer who have consistently produced inexpensive wines are better value for money than those who have suddenly decided to dump their less than fine wine in the UK. Other names to look out for include Bel Arbors, Cartlidge and Brown Stratford. Of course if you can afford the money the best Californian wines are very good indeed.

California has always produced sparkling wines, but in recent years some of the French Champagne houses have been buying their own vineyards or joining forces with existing growers to produce a new wave of sparkling wines. Priced at £10.00-13.00 plus they are under-cutting the traditional celebration fizz by a significant amount. They are well worth a try for a special occasion. Names to look out for include Maison Deutz, Cuvée Napa Valley and Carneros.

Organic wine seems to be the latest trend with Fetzer introducing two new wines produced from organically grown grapes. Whether this is a fashionable fad or a lasting phenomenon remains to be seen. Another new development in California is the creation of specific appellations within the larger wine producing areas, such as the Nappa and Sonoma valleys. So far, four areas, including Stag's Leap, have been given this special status. Such differentiation will probably add even more to the price of these wines.

Another possible trend is a move away from long maturing Cabernet Sauvignon to Merlot and Zinfandel. These two grape varieties are capable of producing very drinkable wines much more quickly than the traditional Cabernet and the Californians are waking up to the fact that not everyone wants to wait 10 years or more for their wines to mature.

South America

Chile is the first of what promises to be a number of South American success stories. Introduced for the first time only a few years ago we are now buying more than three million bottles a year and this could double again in the next few years.

Thanks to the desire of the Chilean government for foreign currency, prices remain reasonable. Supermarket own-label wines will only set you back about £3.50-4.00 and a good many wines fall below the £5.00 limit I have set for this book.

News from Argentina shows that their wine production is not yet as advanced as in Chile. There is enormous potential but improvements have been slow. A few Argentine wines are starting to find their way onto the high street wine shelves but progress is slow.

Brazilian wine, too, have appeared in Britain but there are very few in the supermarkets. The best come mainly from the Palomas winery which is situated almost on the border with Uruguay. This area is much drier than the traditional vine-growing areas and has less of a problem with rot. In some areas the grapes are so drenched in bright blue copper sulphate chemicals that they have to be washed before being crushed and made into wine!

Even Peru is sometimes represented on the supermarket shelves. So for sheer novelty look out for one of these wines to serve next time you have friends round for a meal.

Chile

After a few bumps and hiccups, Chilean wine seems to have settled down. It is no longer just a fashionable wine fad but has become a good buy. At first the range of wine on offer was not as wide as that from Australia but the prices were extremely competitive. Today choice is on the increase as Merlot wines join Cabernet Sauvignon and Riesling and Gewürztraminer join Sauvignon Blanc and Chardonnay. Experimental work is also going on with

Pinot Noir, Sangiovese, Nebbiolo, Syrah and Zinfandel.

Of course, Chilean wine can be as variable as the wine from any other country, but the introduction of stainless steel fermenters and small oak barrels means that it is becoming much more consistent. Added to this is the infectious enthusiasm and growing expertise of the wine-makers. These men are eager not only to improve their wine, but also to produce a style of wine which will appeal to you and me.

The central valley, which runs from north to south between the sea and the Andes, is only 60 to 80 kilometres wide. It has a climate which is eminently suited to raising vines and there is plenty of natural irrigation.

The first vines were introduced from France towards the end of the last century and, thanks to the Andes, they have never been attacked by phylloxera, the dreaded vine louse and so need very little spraying with pesticides. However, yields tend to be high and improvements can be made here.

Sauvignon Blanc predominates among the white wines. On the whole these are crisp and clean but they do not always taste quite how you would expect a Sauvignon Blanc to taste. This may be because of the excessive use of cold fermentation but it may also have something to do with the fact that there is another widely grown but undistinguished grape variety called Sauvignon Vert or Sauvignonasse which may find its way into the mix.

The other problem is that many of the wines are extremely high in alcohol at 13 per cent by volume. As usual the advice is taste before you buy - the best are very good.

There are also some reasonable Chardonnay wines to be found in the supermarkets. On this front new vineyards planted in the Casablanca Valley west of Santiago and close to the cooling Pacific Ocean have been planted with both Chardonnay and Sauvignon and the results look really good.

Cabernet Sauvignon was and still is the mainstay of the Chilean vineyards. On the whole the wines are good but they have the potential to be even better. Merlot has also been planted and is starting to produce some really good wines.

There is no official classification for wines in Chile, though it is claimed that the Agriculture Ministry oversees the monitoring procedures for export wines. All wines are labelled with the grape variety. Each company sets its own standards for basic and Reserva wines. Competition, at least as far as the UK is concerned, is strong and hopefully this should ensure rising standards.

The style of wine is rather more reminiscent of Europe than

of Australia, but the wines do have their own very distinctive varietal flavours. The red wines are matured for a few years before they reach the shops and so even the better wines are usually ready to drink. Some of the Chardonnays are aged in oak barrels to give them a greater depth of flavour. Others are fresh and fruity, but, for me, less interesting.

There are around 12 or more wineries exporting wine from Chile. The best known are probably Concha y Toro, Cousiño Macul, Errazuriz Panequehue and Santa Rita. Less well known but the largest supplier of Chilean white wine to the UK and fourth in size overall is San Pedro. This company supplies a good many own label wines as well as selling under its own labels of Altamiro, Gato and San Pedro. Improvements can probably be expected here now that Jacque Lurton has been called in as international consultant.

Other important contenders in the UK market are Caliterra, Linderos, Montes, Torres, Villard Vineyards and Undurraga Winery. Others worth watching are Santa Emiliana (also part of Concho y Toro, Santa Carolina, Casablanca, Santa Monica for Semillon and Riesling based wines and Valdivieso for sparkling wines.

Argentina

Wine from Argentina is beginning to find its way back into the UK high street, but it does have to overcome memories of the indifferent wine sold in bulk in the sixties, the mediocre sweetish wine in wine boxes in the late seventies and the Falkland conflict against the Argentinians.

Argentina is one of the largest wine-producers in the world, but in the past they have not exported their quality wines. However, this is slowly changing. This is partly because of the involvement of international drinks' companies like Moet and Chandon and partly because the likes of you and me will no longer tolerate the kind of plonk which was around in the sixties. Thanks to the efforts of wine-makers in Australia, Bulgaria, Spain and many other countries, we are used to a very much higher quality even at relatively low prices.

Most Argentine wine in the UK comes from the Mendosa region. This is close to the Andes and is only 160 kilometres as the crow flies from Santiago in Chile. But, because of the Andes, the climate is very different. It is much hotter and drier and the vines are dependent upon irrigation systems.

The potential for good wine from Argentina is enormous. Huge areas are under vine and a large number of different grape varieties are being grown. But, as yet, there are no wine laws and in the vineyard too often quantity is equated with quality. The wineries too need to emulate the kind of investment which has been taking place in Chile.

Wines are labelled by variety and winery. Styles are very variable and some are downright odd. White wines, particularly, are disappointing though wines made from a local variety called Torrentes have a flowery fruitiness which is very attractive. Look out for red wines made with the Malbec grape, they can be very good indeed.

Argentinian wine producers represented over here include Trapiche, Etchart Estates, Weinert and Finca Flichman.

Index